CW00645877

The Inner Woman

ZULMA REYO

Full Court Press
Englewood Cliffs, New Jersey

First Edition

Copyright © 2010 by Zulma Reyo

All rights reserved. No part of this book may be repro-
duced or transmitted in any form or by any means elec-
tronic or mechanical, including by photocopying, by
recording, or by any information storage and retrieval
system, without the express permission of the author
and publisher, except where permitted by law.

Published in the United States of America
by Full Court Press, 601 Palisade Avenue
Englewood Cliffs, NJ 07632

ISBN 978-0-9846113-3-1
Library of Congress Control No. 2010932561

Editing and Book Design by Barry Sheinkopf for Bookshapers
(www.bookshapers.com)

Author photo by Daniel Riera
Cover photo, "Giant Magnolia, Prayer Form," by Barry Sheinkopf

Colophon by Liz Sedlack

DEDICATION

To Daskalos, who opened the way for me.
To Kristos, who reminded me.
And for all the exceptional men who lead our world,
honoring the Feminine Principle within.

TABLE OF CONTENTS

PART TWO: TRAINING AND DEVELOPMENT

APPENDIX

TO ROSINA, MY MOTHER

Mamita...
Do you remember when I was a child
how I would marvel
at the particles of dust
and grains of sand,
at crumbs of bread
and threads of litter
on our carpet floor,
things that no one else could see?
I'd bring you up
upon my little fingertip
without a word!
All I discovered
and treasured,
I wanted you to have!

Today I marvel at
the individual soul,
the feelings in a human heart,
the power of Light
in a second of Love,
the beauty of a smile,
and the flutter of a naked eye,
revealing a magnificence
without a word...!
And I praise you for
the gift of life,

for the joyfulness, the loyalty,
the courage, and the fortitude
that you've inspired,
the eternity you unfold. . .
every moment, every day!

I lay my love, my work,
my life fulfilled
at your feet,
dear heart, reflection of Love/Life shared.

TO ALL WOMEN

THERE IS SO MUCH about being a woman that I want to convey, especially to those women who find themselves misunderstood or too different to fit into the expectations placed upon us. The truth is that our education, regardless of culture, does not take into account the innermost experiential variations between men and women. They are never considered. Apparent differences, even psychological differences, are analyzed, but not the energetic faculties and spiritual consciousness that lead each gender throughout embodiment.

Each woman is a mystery; we know it, we feel it, we live it. So we may as well stop pretending that we aren't. Each man is transparent, analyzable, and somewhat predictable—to *us,* in any event. The love between us calls out for us to honor one another and our differences. I write this book for women and for the men who want to figure us out, although the fact remains that we will not become any clearer or more manageable. We can only acquire the depth, fullness, and life of the mystery herself in dignity and power.

The revelations following states of emotional anguish, fragility, and pain; the sense of fullness beyond displacement, loss, frenzy, and despair; the potent serenity after the raging pit of hopelessness where nothing seems to work and inner and outer reality are wholly disparate entities—these are the ingredients of womanhood. The language is mine, but the spirit, the passionate intensity, is ours. Yours and mine. It is our life song.

I dearly wish that its notes will soothe the roughness of living to yield flowering brightness, that brightness which, as hope, is the Female Principle as she speaks through you and me.

How This Book Came To Be

UNLIKE MY PREVIOUS BOOKS, this one took longer, almost four years, to write and publish in its first version, and then ten more to arrive at its present form. It has been a special love affair. A bittersweet expectancy has filled me throughout. I dared not deal with it directly. It remained concealed all the while as I courted it and was being courted by, it. I wanted it, and yet I didn't want it. I feared I couldn't live up to its beauty and power. I couldn't live up to my self.

Moved by a sense of duty, obligation even, I treaded on in fits and starts, compelled to speak about women in a way that was directly understood by us, in that tone of surreptitious intimacy that is so much our own. Never mind if it wasn't logical or clear, if it was too emotional or romanticized. We understand one another.

As time passed I found a million things to do instead of finishing the book. When I finally gathered up enough courage, in Cyprus in the late winter of '94 another book came through, a study of the construction, energizing, and eventual transformation of thought forms underlying the most common evils that beset both men and women. At the time I didn't see a connection between that very cohesive piece of reasoning and the lovely, poetic, inspirational piece that was being born within me.

So I called for help from "upstairs" and put on my intuitional cap. Mother! *Who* was She? *What* was She, that All-Pervading Female Principle. From the darkest chambers of my depths I summoned MA, the Female Universal Principle, with all my might. The first impression came in the form of the beautiful, radiant lady that I wrote about at the age of nine, who guarded me through loneliness. In my inner experience she was a Golden Lady of Crystal Light, distant but ever present so long ago. I asked Her to guide me now, inspire me, open and show me the way.

At first there was only silence, pregnant with meanings I could not decode. Painfully and not without a fight, I learned to adopt the posture of receptivity and yieldingness it required of me. When my aggressive demand for clarity and detail subsided, in lieu of ascetic gravity I began to hear the still, small voice of Mother's Love within me. Her attitude held me in a field of tenderness and gentle urging that seemed to say, "I am with you. I will help you. Do it."

Do *what?* Her posture was so very different from my own. It was extremely difficult to decode, transmit, or understand the enormous patience and softness that emanated from her as being something useful in today's world.

Then a different image emerged, one filled with the intensity of power and volume. A Cybele. I understood. Life had to be lived in all its depth as well as height, in its darkness as in its light, and the Sublime Mother of all embraced them both. I remembered my teacher Daskalos's touching account of the angel Shamuel, whose immense radiance of Love manifested itself in dimensions of evil in order to entice dark spirits. Once seduced, they would fuse with him to emerge eventually as their original light-filled self once again.

I remembered Mary Magdalene in "Pistis Sofia," the feminine saga. . .she who, as Wisdom, by descending to the lowest planes of creation, is unable to regain her rightful rank in the worlds of Light for aeons of time. There are so many examples of female desolation, abandonment, possession, misery, despair, hope and the calling, over and over again, always searching, returning at long last to that empty place she had never left, to discover that the journey in time was a promise fulfilled: the transmutation of the body of humanity.

Each following thought cast further light upon woman and her many faces, her scars, and her legacy. As above, so below: dark and light, daring and sensitive, Eve and Lillith. Both, as Mother, bridging infinity within space and birthing the forms of the Creator in time, they blended into a single pointed call to women worldwide, saying: Be real. Be sensitive. Dare to use the power of Love, and act dynamically from the sustained experience of yourself.

The book came to life through the pervading stream of Light energy that both aspects, as Mother, irradiated, and which through me have acquired different forms and styles: poems, letters, meditations, and exercises. Given my early Christian upbringing, the Mother's countenance revolved around the scent of Mary Mother and the commanding presence of Mary Magdalene (see Appendix). Combined with my life experiences in observation and in teaching the administration of human life energies as circuits, polarities, and qualities that affect perception, vitality, behavior, and the intimate experience of self, I came to complete my heart's task.

The Love Within Us

I HAVE PUT ASIDE literary and philosophical concerns in addressing myself to women as to a part of myself reaching out to the world of possibility. I have taken pleasure in feeling the words flow through me in the way that God, as the Great Mother, flows and speaks and touches through my form: woman speaking to woman. We have a special way of communicating. It can't be described. It's full of silences, gestures, looks, expressions, quiet movements of the soul and feelings—inner chasms of surging power and ever-billowing yearnings. We know that we know. We also know that we don't know what we know. That is our complicity. It's like a deep, dark secret from the men. They can't figure us out.

As women, love is our teacher and our path. And the ways of love are as endless as the fruits of creation. Love begins with another but it always ends deeply within ourselves as the supreme containing unity. It is our nature. The confusion, suffering, intensities of love in the world train us to *feel* and to discriminate. We discover the laws of being, existing, and creating. . .a feminine world, deep, creative, nourishing, and mysterious. We may witness energies as we ourselves are energy. . .conditioning and being conditioned.

The expression of personality follows our positioning in life, whom we *think* ourselves to be, rather than whom we *feel* ourselves to be. Extremely vulnerable to others' definitions, requirements, and expectations—even if these are concealed—we adopt innumerable guises that do not belong to us. Bringing the personality under the control of individual intelligence is the path tread by learning to love. We seem to learn this by losing ourselves repeatedly, doing and being for another in ways we wouldn't normally do or be for ourselves. Loving, caring, looking after, sympathizing, feeling for others, naturally takes us beyond our own limits. Yet it takes another human being to make this visible and tangible.

Our ways of expressing ourselves through relationship in the world are unequivocally female. Our perception of reality is based on a mechanism of merging and emotional manipulation. Not all women express this in the same way, and not all energize the same lower aspects of the female psyche. Our primal activity is to blend, become complete, and ultimately disappear. I, myself, have developed a remarkable talent for creating conditions and then losing myself in them, claiming to be helpless, when in fact, the power that feeds such helplessness is mine. We also tend to excite easily and deflate much too quickly, being able to inspire, but also to dampen, any entourage.

Intellectual abilities are often shaded by feeling and poetic sentimentality. Sometimes the intellectual effort to match the masculine mind strangles our very nature. My own language is full of overtones of sensation and sensuality. A self-conscious-ness associated with our fine sensibility serves as a magnetic point of attraction. For many, many years, I perceived myself as the center of my world and felt that others were responsible for whatever was happening in me. I felt I was constantly being de-fined from the outside.

Men: We resent them, battle them. . .still we love them and need them to help us to define ourselves and our commonly shared world. Through their being who and what they are, we acquire a framework for the recognition that "I am." They lead our physical world and excel at nobility and youth. And we need to learn humor from them, that light-heartedness in the man-agement of thoughts and concepts that, when they are distin-guished from the emotions, is so artfully theirs.

Being "like" a man for a woman, or being "like" a woman for

a man, even at an early age, has nothing to do with the inner force that our cells impose upon us at a very subtle level. Every woman knows of the abysmal emptiness we carry inside.

Love, as Life, is like a woman. She blends being and becoming in consistently illogical and often uncomfortably seductive ways, mirroring us in our deepest as well as most exalted states. Love is the motor behind life and creation. It has taught me that "I" am in fact the matrix that "I Am"—the space from where I become, and the Consciousness that inhabits the emerging form.

In reality, "I" am something sensed but indefinable, different, yes, definitely different from the men, and with a difference that is essential and functional. This difference caused me despair at times. As they couldn't understand me, I too couldn't understand them—unless there was love. And then explanations are irrelevant: Love is what we *are*.

IN OUR TIME, God, or Absolute Reality, is in truth a masculine principle. The feminine is implied. In manifestation, the two are seen as polar opposites, with a third factor, spirit, understood as the transcendence of both. The difference between common conception and the understanding of this book is subtle but significant. When we speak of the Father here, we do so in the sense of the divine seeding activity that perpetuates life. When the term God is used, it implies the neutral unit beyond all conception.

As in earliest known societies, in this book divinity is perceived as Universal Mother, containing within herself both the feminine principle as well as the masculine principle. Everything in manifestation is seen to revolve around this dual expression, which rather than suggest real persons or roles, illustrates two equal but essentially different and necessary attributes. Male and female. Spirituality and the elevation of the human race as a whole, in this framework, is the result of the return of women to their innermost nature – in other words to the Mother. In this return, the innermost nature of men themselves is awakened. It is the author's belief that this is the sole responsibility of women. No matter what her inclination or style, this is her particular task by virtue of the quality and ability of her gender.

Here, the questions posed by woman reach out through the chaos of her as yet misunderstood inner nature. The guidance of the Universal Mother emerges through the joint voice of two salient archetypes of the Feminine Principle, Mother Mary and the Magdalene. It could just as easily have been Isis, Durga,

Hecate or Bona Dea. Her voice is the Female Principle behind Life.

The following distinctions in meaning are indicated by capitalization or its absence:

Love: *the vibration of universal life pervading all; the expression of Consciousness that triggers movement.*
love: *the human expression of Love as filtered and interpreted personally.*

Being/Beingness: *the essential state of spiritual uniqueness.*
being: *the action of embodying a quality.*

Consciousness: *the state of sublime awareness and intelligence of Beingness as a whole.*
consciousness: *the stepped-down, intelligent awareness of expressions of Consciousness, as in human consciousness, the consciousness of matter, etc.*

Part One

Dialogues
With The Mother

THE CALL

MOTHER!

Where are you?

Help me understand myself!

What is this world all about? I am told to be like this and like that. I am shown how to do this and do that. I am even told what I am or need to be. I think that I am one way, and then I find out that I am another.

Mother, hold me, surround me, remold me. . .fill me with your sweetness, your patience, and your Light! Show me your face that I may know you and, in doing so, find my reflection.

Why is love so many different things? What is this intensity that wells up inside me—this mixture of desires, attractions, and fears? And sex? What are these emotions that seem to devour me? Why is everything so complicated?

Often, I don't know myself apart from another. How can I truly know what I am and what I am not? How can I express, and then communicate, what I am?

How is a man different from me? How does he feel, and think, and sense life? How can I understand him the way he understands himself? How can he come to understand me the way I am and feel? How can he comprehend these forces that yield and manifest, absorb and radiate, that go infinitely within and infinitely without?

THE ANSWER

DAUGHTER!

My little girl of purity and innocence,
daughter of starlight and of the night,
my passionate child of tears and joy,
I have always been here!
I have always loved you and followed you.
But my words are softness, and my body is your own.
Your feelings are my actions,
and your blood is my life!
I have been waiting for your call.

Worlds are born within me and unfold.
I am this and I am that. . .in a continuous now.
I have no boundaries, and I am all boundaries.
I know everything, and I know nothing.
I am all feelings.
I am the depths of virginity
embracing seeds in time.
Between my breasts I hold man
and feed him with my own life
that he may know me and, in knowing me,
honor me in his world.

To know me,
you had to lose whom you believed you were
and reach for me, my Love!
You had to make space within space,

for I am the body of absolute infinite Beingness,
the heart-pulse of endless Love and Life,
the unborn possibility of Life
within the darkness that contains the Light.
I am one: your unified embrace around the Earth,
daughter of the future splendor of all Life.

I am Hope.

LETTER ONE: WHO AM I?

My Love,

You will be surprised, precious daughter, that in these letters to you I will not dwell upon your personal identity or *specific* situations in the physical world. If I seem at times to ignore your problems with friends and lovers, with relationships, with your career—or with all those psychological issues that seem so important, and are important to *you*—it is because you already have too many answers. There are thousands and thousands of books that will help you understand the sequence of events that bring about typical life frustrations. For every effect, there is a cause, and these are endless!

There are scant sources that will give you what I can. Few will point you to what you are and awaken you to yourself as a real woman, which you already are at the inner levels. Only this will allow you to link what you feel with possible expressions, what you know with what is probable.

I wish you to be yourself, so I offer you sketches. Upon them you may elaborate your image and reflection to suit the situation. Merging with me, you will find nourishment. Solutions arise as a result of Being. They follow your fullness. It is something that *happens*, not something that is done. Learn to read the signs.

These letters are about *what* you are. There are too many people telling you *who* you are and who you ought to be.

LETTER TWO: WHAT AM I?

Daughter of Light,

It is important that you explore life as only you can, through your femininity. Being woman is a very special state of knowing and being. The Female Principle dwells beneath all appearances as the unity of life. Through your instinctively felt understanding, you will reach the intuitive intelligence of the heart.

The eternal feminine might be defined as the force of containing-within-itself out of which the cycles of creation emerge, to express through movement what exists as latent being. Woman is the embracing capacity of God in our minds, our bodies, and our psyches.

Ours is the hollowness within all form. The proverbial symbol of woman—the cauldron, or the pot—conveys that all-containing function that we serve. Our minds operate on the principle of wordless understanding. Our personalities express this as emotional love, and our bodies' substance provides the textures for creation on many, many levels. Our every expression is in fact a birthing in each of our worlds or dimensions.

Our hollowness in matter, as a womb, allows us to absorb and gestate. Out of the mind of the feminine, the substance of creation arises. You emanate from yourself, physically and emotionally, the seeded power of the Mother, the holy source and primal substance of creation. You are the custodian of this holy spiritual power.

Much depends upon your becoming whole again, uniting outer expression with the spirit of the Mother. Much depends too on your positioning, which must always be in essence, in emptiness. The trick is to learn how to do this and still be part of the world, still assume your responsibilities, still enjoy the game of appearance, sensation, and endless weaving of experience.

Everyone dreams of a better world, a world of peace, but few know what this means. Imagine the turbulence and tension of war. Now imagine containing it all within a mantle of Light. Conceive of holding, *sustaining*, that state. The intensity that holds the world together, this is peace, the coexistence of opposites. It is not yet transcendence, but the state just prior to it. It is the Female Principle at work. It can only happen when the subject is wholly removed from identification with form. This is our life's task.

Letter Three: Is There Such A Thing As Pure Feeling?

Beloved Harmonizer,

Feelings are the result of our sense experience of another part of life. The parts within this relationship can be perceived as harmonious or discordant. You are both energizer and witness. Your feeling nature predominates over the abstraction of your absorbent mind. When you sense agitation, such as fear, unease, or discomfort, your tendency will be to either add to it or allow yourself to be sucked in by it. In either case, you believe you are "feeling" and lose sight of what you are witnessing. True feeling is *witnessing*, devoid of interpretation or involvement.

Humankind has forgotten how to relate heart to heart. Relationships are handled, remolded, administered, and negotiated. People function almost exclusively through the Male Principle—i.e., the efficiency and management of form. This enslaves both genders to the world of appearances. It is not the male perspective that is wrong; it is the fact that one excludes the other. Form overwhelms quality. As a result, men suffer from the inability to be themselves in the right measure of flexibility and softness. And women are rarely able to exert the appropriate quantum of attraction and containment in leadership.

Screaming, crying, pouting, or repressing accomplish nothing. Neither do guilt or self-pity, anger, sadness, or defeatism. These so-called feelings settle into fixations that can only be undone by changing yourself radically. And I don't mean through logic or reason.

Men tend to conclude through reasoning rather than reason through feeling. Unwilling to feel reality emotionally, they place the cart before the horse and construct the content—in other words, the feelings—to fit the forms or systems they build mentally. This is not feeling but *interpretation*. Women go crazy with this and drive men even crazier when they use the same process chaotically, as *their* nature will have it.

What happened to truly spontaneous human experience, a spontaneity that is meant to spice, accompany, and support discernment of intelligent feeling? We live in a universe of shifting perspectives and continuous movement. You can capture feelings no more than you can prevent their occurrence. The only thing you can control is your reaction to them. For this to be appropriate, you would have first to be aware of what the feelings are, without a label, as pure experience.

When you awaken to this state of the art through the right combination and exercise of feeling and reason, you can as a woman incarnate the Feminine Principle that contains the male as seed within. And men can embody the Male Principle, engulfing the female qualities around its power core.

LETTER FOUR: WHY IS FEELING
OFTEN PAINFUL?

My Feeling Heart,

We are speaking of emotions, the infinite levels and motions of Love. They are both a treasure and a curse, depending on how we handle them.

Through your emotions, you are connected with the subtlest resonances of feeling. This sensitivity is expressed in your physical self as sensation, your emotional self as feeling, and in the mental realm as the awareness of cognition. To resist or deny your sensitivity implies disconnection. Disconnection leads to more pressure and chaos when the forces we are meant to handle brew uncontrolled.

There is not a woman in the world who does not instinctively respond to the cry of vulnerability from a living thing. And yet there are many women who have been conditioned into insensitivity, who respond more imminently to concepts than to the direct experience of life. Everywhere upon the face of this planet, children—black, white, yellow, red, or brown—are weeping. They call for your embrace in a very physical and tangible way. This means touching and holding, caressing and feeling together with them, in the flesh.

Nature made it so that you remain etherically linked* to your offspring throughout their lifetimes. Your children's bodies and personalities are constructed out of your substance, and you are attuned to them as to your own. God also made it so

---

* *"Ether" should not be confused with psychic or astral light, it is a kind of pre-material intelligent substance between the state of Consciousness and gross matter, which constitutes the blueprint for physical form.*

that, as Her image and faculties of expression, you are spiritually linked with *all* of humanity. As spiritual mothers you are her knowingness, a pervading state of knowing, as Consciousness with a capital "C".

It is no surprise that you can no longer ignore the world situation in cozy gardens of self-indulgence. Look into the eyes of a small child. Can you truthfully believe that this child is better, or worse, than another? Can you close the door to what you feel? Pain brings awakening, healing, and forgiveness. It is your presence clothed in the female psyche that will change the past. Rather, go into the future as the living image of affection in the hearts of your children. It is time for real motherhood. Where else can She express herself if not through you and in your world, your thoughts, your feelings, your actions, your home, and your dreams?

Instead of licking your wounds in a self-centered attempt to attract others to you, reveal the essential woman who understands because she loves, who loves because she vibrates in resonance with her self. This is the sisterhood that breeds integrity and humility, and that opens the door to the excellence of realization, good will, patience, and discernment. The Mother is longing to contain her children within the warm folds of your feeling womb. There, in the warmth of love, she will heal and inspire the world.

Feeling is not painful. Become aware of what truly hurts as you allow your heart to expand!

LETTER FIVE: CAN LOVE BE WASTED?

Tender Love,

Essentially, Love is a state of Consciousness that emits a particular substance. Hence it is both Intelligence as well as form. The state of Being-Love is quite different from the act or thought of loving. This state affects the energies of the human being and actually produces a subtle substance that regenerates, heals, and does a lot more at many levels, including affecting the mind and surrounding people and things. Until you are strong and tested in the ways of the world, the activity of this substance, and the force it emits, are experienced as emotions creating harmony or havoc.

Feelings are not things. They are movements, perceived by us, to do with and express as we see fit. We decode or interpret them in a number of ways. Of course it is possible to misuse the energy generated in us. Learning constructive ways of handling this emotional force is the highest science of womanhood.

The greatest misplacement of emotional force comes through self-indulgent excesses, in other words, wrong motivation and expectation. At these times, we handle emotions as if they were currency and trade in them indiscriminately.

Observe yourself. Bring to mind those times when you feel spent after an especially intense emotional upheaval. Remember the feeling just above the pit of the stomach, followed by the quivers, the gnawing sensation that accompanies exhaustion, frustration, and the sense of lack of protection or danger that remains. It is an indication that you have gone beyond ordinary limits—a sure sign that you have not known when to stop. Then you question the value of your feelings, your love.

If you feel the ingratitude of others, it is because you expected appreciation for your efforts. If you feel misunderstood, it is because you demanded understanding in return. If nobody seems to care, it is because you don't care enough to stand whole in yourself and look to another to reflect your wholeness to you. As most impulsive and automatic emotional involvements tend to be, it was a commercial transaction.

With the tremendous sensitivity our nature brings to us comes also the *capacity to feel all that is not love.* Only if we are physically and psychologically stable and harmonious—full of the feeling of Self—can we possibly counterbalance the perception of the negative-feeling world around us in order to make a difference. This is especially true because we feel through the sensations of our own bodies.

Understand your motivations. We tend to leave the doors of our house (our body) wide open to intruders all the time. Instead of being irradiators, we draw inside ourselves the energy that is around us. It is the female brand of indolence. Either through investment or through melodrama, the result of indiscriminate feeling is to end up feeling spent. And here the negative influence of the subconscious forces that surround our depths takes over, and we are urgently forced to learn psychic self-defence.

To be open, trusting, and loving all the time is unintelligent. There is no escaping the anguish that follows the promiscuous and unguarded use of one's energies. You set the stage for fear, rejection, and worthlessness as you try to sell a deficient product. There is nothing attractive about a gaping hole. Who in his right mind will love someone who doesn't love herself, someone who is needy and empty? Our own fuzziness and lethargic kind of loving, devoid of real presence, is an open invitation for negativity. When, on the other hand, we are filled with the presence of Self, we don't seek explosive or vampirizing people and situations. Our own bodies' feelings guide us.

Learn to distinguish the spiritual force of Love, which uses your personality, from the emotional response that follows your selfish involvements in the world. The latter uses and abuses your physical vitality; the former adds to it. You may believe you are *open* and *giving*, but is your vital energy sufficiently full to back up your intent? Most often you are in want and automatically draw in kind from others. In the worst scenario, you attract what you reject or fear the most.

Love is qualified and bestowed through acts in a measure and guise appropriate to the circumstance. Many people can only accept it in very small doses. Respectfully acknowledge this. Love is appropriateness itself. If you go beyond the natural barriers people put up, you pay for it with energy depletion and disappointment.

You may withhold the physical expression of love, but never the awareness of the feeling you have inside. Learn to modify your expressions to suit the other's capacity without diminishing inner feeling, the invisible emission of that love which is a source of healing. Instead of seeking recognition, take pleasure in simply feeling for feeling's sake.

Your power to attract whatever is necessary in the world grows according to your capacity to sustain love unselfishly. This means acquiring holding power. It entails being able to pool love's resources just as you would money in the bank. If you spend it as quickly as you get it, you will never have very much and you will never be able to afford bigger and greater things. When you know you are plentiful and trust your holding power, then you will know the feeling of abundance at every level.

Never regret or be ashamed of love or of shedding a tear. Real love is never wasted. It is never lost or consumed, because it comes from surplus. Love doesn't come *from* you; as a substance, it comes *through* you. . .requiring your conscious acceptance and unselfish emission to become the inspiring constructive force for good in the world.

LETTER SIX: HOW CAN I DISTINGUISH REALITY FROM MY DESIRES, MEMORIES, AND EXPECTATIONS?

Dearest One,

This is fundamental. In the world, every woman must be a keen observer. If you set yourself to it, there is very little that can escape your eye. You must develop your already-intuitive perception by training in observation, discrimination, and patience.

Understand: You possess two great powerhouses of force. Both are inner. One is an energetic frequency that attracts and fecundates substance directly—is, in other words, a birthing power for creation of all sorts. The other is an emission that is capable of awakening levels of consciousness. The first power relates to your body. It affects matter as well as emotional and mental forms. All are nourished by this natural emission of yours as guardian of the etheric fluid* that produces substance.

The second powerhouse concerns the way in which you express yourself. It is a frequency of non-linear intelligence capable, not only of inspiring, but also of raising levels of consciousness. Men depend on this female force to fulfil their natural role as those who evoke, sustain, and effectively implement Consciousness in the world. The divine feminine polarity draws energies into expression, contains them, and also generates them from the inner realms.

---

*etheric fluid: A subtle force that has the quality, i.e. texture, of substance between the gas and liquid state; invisible to ordinary perception, it is similar to the 19th century notion of "ectoplasm" and may be tangibly sensed with appropriate training.

Woman is responsible for the emanations that project themselves at the heart. These may trigger either illumination or its opposite. For this reason, you must learn to discern between essence and appearance, and to guard against empowering selfish or negative forms.

Notice how you feed your desires and projections. Your will, as indirectly activated subconscious power, was the force misused by black witches in the past. You can sustain the intensities of desire so well that you are capable of forcing persons and situations to embody your projection. With little awareness, you do this with men. You do it with your children, with situations in the immediate world around you impregnated with your beliefs and colored by your likes and dislikes.

Depth observation of your own feelings and desires is, therefore, critical for you. This implies a distancing, but one that cannot be devoid of sensitivity. Instead, your emotional nature should be harnessed by intelligence—the non-linear variety that issues from the heart.

Desires, memories, and expectations are thoughts that have been animated with emotional force. To deflate them, you need to work on two fronts: that of the mind, and that of the emotions. Once you understand what you propose to transform, you must set out to harness and redirect the force. Resistance to your impulses does not imply denial. It requires a watchful, feeling state.

Remember that you attract whatever vibrates* at the same frequency you do, whether at the level of emotion or of con-

---

*vibration: resonance experienced in the body and its surrounding space as pulsation responding to the composition of the body-mind-emotion of an individual. It is similar to the sound perception from a tuning-fork, streaming into a fine extension of progressively finer wavelets.

sciousness. Although grasped through the same feeling faculty, spiritual consciousness is very different from emotion. In order to perceive in consciousness, you must look beyond your own likes and dislikes, your own attitudes toward right and wrong in life.

Then you will know what is real—direct experience beyond polarity. Your positioning in the fullness of time will reveal everything. There is no longer confusion.

LETTER SEVEN: HOW DO I CORRECTLY HANDLE
MY ABILITY TO ATTRACT PEOPLE AND CONDITIONS?

My Lightbearer,

You are built in such a way that you do indeed attract people and conditions to you. This is not always visible. You may try to make yourself invisible or cover yourself up, as women have in the past, but you are built this way, and there is nothing you can do to change it. It places a great deal of responsibility on you, as you will see. Whether you are aware of it or not, your presence alone will change the energy configuration of the world around you. This is not sufficiently understood or accepted.

Your obvious polarity is magnetic, yet you embody two distinct functions on two different levels. You attract in order to bestow. Outwardly, you are magnetic and attractive; inwardly, you are electric and giving. You are aware of the first but not of the second.

As emptiness and as a container of all that is, it is not in your inner nature to say *no*. As an attractive center of irradiating force, it is not in your outer nature to say *yes*. In fact there is nothing about you that can be defined! Understand both these reactions, and go beyond them. Learn to say *yes* and to say *no* with strength and conviction. You will come to know the real from the imitations and pretentions within yourself and others only when you have been weathered through trial and error.

Unlike your brother, who is monofocused, it is easy for you to become sidetracked. This is all the more reason why you must learn to carry through with decisions to balance your essential flexibility—which doesn't mean to say that you must become rigid. Living as we do in the inner whirlpool of events, we desist much too easily from things men consider important.

Men, in their capacity to use psychic mind-substance*, are limited by their insistence upon form. Unless a man has known and embraced within himself the hollowness that woman is, his constructions will be shallow, practical, graceful, and aesthetic at best. . .but not inspirational. On the other hand, when in love, his creations are sublime because he immerses himself in the Female Principle and transcends gender.

Women, through their insistence upon content, find it difficult to pursue an objective if it means ignoring all the "little" things that matter to them, but when in love they embrace the *Male* Principle. When she becomes protective, she can be as goal-oriented and monofocused as any man, and elevate everything and everyone surrounding her. She becomes inspirational and clear, didactic and useful, because she transcends the limitation of gender.

Don't allow defeat or bitterness to overshadow you. You are the Light bearer of the future. What you think will come to pass. This is the mighty power of the feminine mind as it casts a die upon the mold of etheric feeling, applying the emotional resonance that coaxes physical, material form into reality.

If you do not honor who you are, you will be unable—by energetic law—to attract any person or situation in which you will be honored and can be honorable. Any neediness or lack in the other will mirror your own, and the relationship, as you now know, turn into barter. This is not what you are about.

Let your every action, be it giving or receiving, be a con-

---

*mind-substance: *The frequency or vibration that resonates at the level of thought conditioned by emotional affinity, and that determines its shape and quality.*

scious *acknowledgement* of Love's substance.* As you value your-self, you will come to value others and distinguish what is of value.

Become aware of the dynamic of cause and effect that is re-vealed when you set personal emotions aside and are guided from within. Then your actions will be impregnated with power rather than whim, and result in intelligent decisions based on both power and insight.

---

*Love's substance: If we understand Love as a state of Being, the resonance resulting from this state suffuses a balancing quality through whatever surrounds it, much like harmonizing, healing, soothing waves.

LETTER EIGHT: WHY CAN'T MEN UNDERSTAND ME? IT ALWAYS SEEMS THAT ONE IS RIGHT AND THE OTHER WRONG. WHY CAN'T LOVE HEAL OUR DIFFERENCES?

My Idealistic Child,

You are *both* "right." And perfect. But you are more perfect in your differences.

We understand what we are. We can never understand what we are not. At the most, we can accept it. The power we hold as magnetic centers of attraction—something unknowable and un-controllable—has caused men to revere and abhor us at the same time through the ages. Electricity and magnetism do not fuse. Like water and fire in alchemy, they are distinct creative forces that work in realms beyond themselves.

Education and social conditioning are mere veneer. Under-neath, the sexes compete with one another. There are millions of years of conflict and pain behind us to back up the mistrust we have cultivated for one another, a phenomenon that goes be-yond what love can contain, a fear that has existed as long as the separation of the sexes. At the level of physical expression it is the *sine qua non* of the human condition. The realms of fusion and perfection are not of this world.

The task of both men and women is to *live* in the light of inner values and perfection while *performing* on the stage of ap-pearances and imperfection: to hold the peace, that is, while liv-ing in conflict.

Men are natural doers, creators, constructors, and leaders in the world. Although we share in all these activities, *our* doing, creating, constructing, and leading in the world are inclined to-wards quality and inner experience.

Women are susceptible to, and often obliged to uphold, many conditions in the intellectual, concrete world that seem to require a denial of our feeling nature. We are fundamentally receptive and dwell deep within the fluid faculty of feeling and perception, so it is difficult to communicate accurately who and what we are, what we think or desire, or how to hold our ground conceptually. This is why, against your better judgment, you often find yourself competing with men or straining to please or think like them. If you don't become aggressive yourself, you become defensive. It is difficult to be as you are without feeling that something is wrong with you. *Emotionally*, men experience the same frustration.

Our bodies express identical human faculties, and our minds behold the same outer reality. But men and women perceive and respond differently. Woman's way of relating with, and in, the world is through a fine mechanism of inner attunement, men's through a complex of subtle assessments and calculations. Women absorb everything from our environment— ideas, feelings, and forces—in a way that is similar to the indelible process of photography. We retain what we see physically, emotionally, and mentally. We never forget. Instead, men excel in the world of possibilities and often ignore the here-and-now.

We are natural perceivers and amplifiers of energy and force. Unchecked, this faculty automatically feeds into our emotions and, in turn, appropriates everything that surrounds us. We believe what we are told by men, whose mounting frustration is that they can neither control nor predict us. They have told us that our emotions and our sex are the cause of the evil unleashed in the world. We have even been led to believe we are the cause of original sin. We are still reaping the consequences of this assertion. We are charged with subconscious guilt that only serves to exacerbate possessiveness and paranoia—all because of magnetism and electricity.

We are taught to handle ideas in the same way as males. We learn to debate and to compete, to formulate and to abstract, in identical ways. But our thinking is intuitive; we *feel* rather than *see* ideas. This intuitive conceptualizing capacity is wider than men's and offers us more breadth of insight although not always as much precision and detail. We may come to excel in objective reasoning, but it doesn't come easily for most of us. At best we experience a kind of objective subjectivity, a perception from the innermost core of Being. We are a constant becoming.

My daughter, there is *nothing to heal* here. Differences are differences. Instead, honor and respect whatever is different from you as it helps you to be you.

As women, we feel who, or rather *what*, we are. Yet we constantly insist on definition. All too often we ask someone to tell us how we look—not out of insecurity, but because we do not have a firm sense of form, as men do. This also applies to emotions. It may also come as a surprise that jealousy is not a natural condition for woman. Our real nature, rather, is to draw into ourselves in order to hold, to cherish, and to nourish all that lives, breathes, and pulsates —all of God's creation. At its core, this instinctive activity is devoid of ownership, exclusion, or envy.

We are instinctively courageous regarding the emotions. Our somewhat reckless spirit in this respect can become a source of conflict for others, especially men. We explore emotions as easily as clothing, acquiring shape after shape of movement within them. We actually enjoy experiencing the perpetual shifting that brings meaning to us. Our thinking reflects this, replete with sensuous, intense imagery.

Our *way* of thinking gives us an innate ability to reach up into the higher dimensional realms of mind. We know what an idea or a concept *feels* like. We may not always be able to translate this into concrete terms without help from men—this way of thinking that defines our common world.

Rather, therefore, than ask why men cannot understand you, it is your place to understand them while holding onto your truth.

LETTER NINE: HOW TO COMMUNICATE EFFECTIVELY
WHAT I KNOW INTUITIVELY?

Ancient One,

We have had the same problem for the last 2,000 years and more. We have transmitted who and what we are through silence and mystery, preserving, healing, and embracing humanity, all the while wading through the interpretations cast over us. It has been something of a losing battle. Now is the time to deal with detail at every level. The reconstruction of the world depends on it, and on our ability to use the word.

Your question has to do with the use of the concrete mind when perception is attained through subjective, intuitive channels. We are able to prove our point once we master reasoning, but we are incapable of transmitting the wisdom attained by non-verbal means through sequential thinking. Just as we have to embrace the Male Principle, men have to embrace the Female Principle for any depth of communication to be possible.

For women, the process begins by isolating and studying perception from both levels before attempting to bridge the sensitivity of the body—feelings network with the machinery of the thinking mind. In other words, you must be grounded in your emotions. The trick is to develop reason without harming this delicate mechanism. In ancient times, women were educated exclusively among women and protected from the forces that might jeopardize sensitivity and imagination.

Untrained, women tend to be woolly thinkers, and some women never make any sense at all in a man's world. Not all women feel the calling or need to develop debating or verbal communication skills. In the right measure, and for those women who set themselves to it, thinking serves to discipline and enhance an emotional nature. Trained, women make excellent practical and humane philosophers and leaders, as we are witnessing today.

We meet men at the level of abstraction, and it is from there that we reach the higher aspect of mind together, and can lead them to the realm of spirit through the true intelligence of heart.

To understand and blend with us in creative dimensions of Being, men go through the process in inverse order. *They* begin, by employing their minds, to survive the agonizing marshes of emotions. *We* begin with the emotions, and we strive painfully to harness our spirit as we come to discipline our minds. The intuitional backdrop of our ordinary thinking is forever present. Our mind is always functioning on two levels.

Originally, Beingness*, which embraces a lot more than our conception of God, was conceived as feminine—Mother—and held the triune power of engendering, creating, and preserving. Everything—substance, form, faculty, and power— was born of Her. The Kogis of South America, akin to the Australian aborigines, call the state of mind in which everything exists simultaneously *Aluna*. In Sanskrit She is called *Prakriti*. This is both a state of Being as intelligence, and the spontaneous activity emanating from that state of Being. The emanation is the Light substance from which the fabric of matter arises. For us to comprehend this state, we need to fine-tune ourselves. This implies raising our frequency level.

Attunement (i.e., blending with the energy of, or "falling in

---

Beingness: The state of Being that connotes essence. In this case, godliness or the absolute whole.

tune" with, another) is a particular way of using the mind. It's like centering ourselves in the experience of the thought itself. This is non-directional. We do not project *towards* but rather emerge *from* that state. There is, in fact, no process. It is instantaneous. Our mind, the female mind, works this way. Consider the phenomenon of peace. Only one who is actually peaceful can instil that energy; no amount of doing will produce what the state of Being achieves instantly. Very young children speak that language of Being.

We perceive, and we participate in what we perceive, simultaneously. This means that our mental activity empowers rather than defines. The defining, or "doing," dynamic corresponds to the male mind. Both female and male modalities compose our normal thinking and feeling abilities.

The ancients did not waste resources. They did not pursue explanations that could only be found in feeling experience through logical, sequential thinking, and vice-versa. This is how Mystery Schools arose. Today we use questioning intelligence for things that do not require it. In fact, intelligence is equated with questioning and evaluation rather than with pure perception.

Women's vision of life—like that of the ancients who knew of Beingness beyond the tangible—is simple, humanitarian, and ecological. But it is a lifestyle that does not make us wealthy, important, powerful, or special. We are obliged to consider the whole rather than the particular at all times. Rather than exert force, it yields. It communicates through harmony, honoring the rhythms, cycles, and dictates of nature.

This is how we may become masters over creation substance: alchemists. But that is another subject.

LETTER TEN: HOW CAN PSYCHOLOGY HELP ME?

Daughter of Life,

You should rather ask how *you* could help psychology!

Psychology is an optimal way of using the linear mind and its extension, the abstract mind. In its current form it allows us to organize and make sense of ourselves and of those impressions we sense from our surroundings. It helps us to construct our identity and assure the independence that is the foundation of real collaboration.

In our shared culture, we learn to part from a definition of ourselves. Psychology trains us to focus and move great blocks of feeling energy, alone and in combination. It is the mathematics and geometry of human behavior. As women, we swim through this like fish in water.

It is important that we do not confuse who or what we *are* with the identity we *construct*. Personality expresses our true individuality, but when we act from a definition rather than an experience it becomes egoism. Many schools of psychology deal with labels rather than content, with adjustment rather than with self-discovery. They do not always make a distinction between what pertains to thinking and what to feeling.

Like everything else in this world, egoism has male and female styles. Whereas the tendency in men is to distort reality by constructing mental screens and exercising thought forms that support their vested interests, women pollute the milieu with emotional mismanagement of energy currents in the name of thinking. To satisfy the need for feedback from the outside, we emanate emotional thought forms that qualitatively alter our surroundings. Our selfishness expands and agitates, or it contracts and withdraws.

We are inclined to leech onto whatever will give us boundaries. "Who am I?" becomes "*What* am I?" This quickly translates into "How am I?" or, better still, "What do I *do*?" Before you know it, you have contorted yourself to fit into the prevailingly male mind mold. Eventually out of control, you ask, "What is happening?" as if it had nothing to do with you! This is how our particular brand of madness hides behind confusion, wooliness, and sentimentality. Avoiding this pattern of behavior, we can picture the hardness and toughness that negates the feminine soul.

To be truly useful in a better world, psychology must also clearly draw the line between emotion, sentiment, and love.

Ordinary emotions are basically egocentric. They bind the receiver to the sender like glue, travelling great distances to achieve this, involving things, places, and people in the personal meaning and history of the subject. Sentiment goes a step further, relating to idealized, more stereotyped feeling, color-coded to the manipulative bent of the originator.

Love is different. It is neither emotional nor sentimental. It is an extension of the fullness of Being*. Learning to transmute

---

*fullness of Being: The real self or essence made conscious of its Being state. In regard to essence vs. Being, as far as the personality is concerned they are synonymous. Concerning the dynamic of creation, essence addresses a pre-Being state; Being points to the primordial individual spark. Another person or situation may inspire it, but the influence ends there. It is a wholly impersonal, liberating and uplifting irradiation that does not bind but rather blends one whole with another, comprising a core of essence that represents both.

emotional charge into a freeing love force comprises the skill that a realized woman learns as she masters her feeling nature through the refinement process of intelligence, an intelligence that goes beyond the scope of current psychology and reaches directly into the realms of the Mother.

LETTER ELEVEN: EXPLAIN THE DIFFERENCE BETWEEN SENSUALITY AND SEXUALITY—IS IT DIFFERENT FOR MEN?

My Sensuous Girl,

Basically, women are sensual and men are sexual. Sensuality and sexuality are intimately related, but they can also be mutually exclusive.

Allowed to develop naturally, women's every breath is an ecstatic experiment of feeling and sensing delight. We enjoy finer beyond-the-body frequencies with almost equal pleasure. Don't ever feel ashamed of enjoying the sensations of life, physical, emotional, or spiritual. You were made to dance with the stars and flow with the waters of creation. Sensuality is as foundational in you as it is in the newborn infant who delights in the bath water, or the puppy at the seashore chasing waves for the sheer pleasure of moving.

Sensuality relates to the joy of living life wholly. It is the way the senses express themselves when they are full and vibrant. Although it is induced by, and satisfies, sensation, it involves and transcends *all* the senses. This includes hearing, smelling, and, most certainly, feeling.

There is a great difference between sensuality and sexuality, usually targeted towards the satisfaction of a craving. This craving suggests a cycle of yearning, absorption, and satiety. On the other hand, sensuality is a continuous state of being in which one takes pleasure in experiencing without ulterior motive or saturation point. When sensuality becomes the means to an end, it turns into sexuality.

Observe the physical difference between the genders. The masculine body manifests a thrust forward into action. The feminine body demonstrates attraction and containment. This does not relate to behavioral patterns of extroversion or introversion, but to energy modality.

Men divide and conquer, analyze and segment life into constituent parts and reorder them into areas and categories. They pass from one activity to another effortlessly. Women cannot disconnect so readily, which is why we can't forget easily. We accumulate and augment. Our physical expression is the same as our emotional. It is difficult for us to respond to only one part, say the genitals, without triggering an entire bodily need that automatically translates as emotional as well. Our language is enfoldment and adaptation. We embrace our man physically, emotionally, mentally, and psychically.

We feel obligated to have sex when we do not crave it. We yearn for the fullness of communion but settle for whatever we can get.

At these times we *think* our body into response, and if this doesn't work, we fake it. Our tolerance levels to sensory stimuli tend to be considerably higher than men's. We can withstand greater amounts of joy as well as pain, as in childbirth. Under the right emotional and spiritual conditions, our bodies ignite instantly and fully. We treasure being appreciated for who and what we are rather than for what we appear to be and how we please another. Actually, what turns us on the most is emotional appreciation and reciprocity.

This does not mean that there are not women who respond strongly to the basic sexual instinct. However, expectations are such today that too many lie in order to convince themselves and the other that they fit the norm. They perform tricks to excite themselves and reach orgasm, often initiating and finishing the job for themselves. Once hooked into any device, including mental stimulation, true responsiveness is severely impaired. And behind that kind of self-induced excitement, devoid of depth, lurks a shadow of resentment that grows and grows.

Nobody is truly asexual, yet many women who tread the spiritual path consider themselves that today, simply because they do not respond to time pressures and segmentation. *Understand how you respond to all of life.* Resist peer and cultural pressures. Be who and what you are. Communicate who you are *as you are.*

Most sexual training overstresses technique, starving and violating your delicate, subtle mechanisms. Be still. Be still *together with your partner.* And *know.* Be delicate and sensitive and share with your lover. Enter the body temple together, in purity and wholeness. Nothing less than that will do for you.

You do not *need* anyone or anything. Men need us more than we need them. If you are not in a relationship, ask yourself if you really want one. Learn patience with discrimination, and then be what you wish to attract. You will attract what you are. Refine yourself. Work out your psychological desires, filters, and interpretative mechanisms, including your obsessions or preoccupations about being in relationship and having children. Not everybody is designed the same way!

Above all, delight in your body, naturally, serenely, invisibly, just for you. You respond exuberantly to natural cycles. At these times you hardly know what to do with the intensities you experience. Find creative ways of sharing that energy as joy and inspiration, as gratitude to life and for being alive. This is the Mother's gift of love to you. Take advantage of it and use it wisely.

Letter Twelve: How To Choose Between Sexual Attraction And Spiritual Yearning?

My Nourishing Girl,

There is no choice to be made when we are concerned with experience.

You are always in relationship, whether it is exclusive and intimate or within typical social interchange boundaries. To a greater or lesser extent, relationship implies sharing a life path, inspiring, lifting, and helping one another to reach inner realization. We do this with friends as with sexual partners and children. Spirituality flourishes in the ground set by relationships. Imposed aloneness creates imbalance. Whereas it is impossible to be alone, it *is* possible to be "all-one."

Far from satisfying one another's expectations and always seeking a good time, relationship, like all spiritual work, does not come gratuitously; it implies sacrifice. When you are convinced that you are incomplete and lacking in worth, then giving to another is an obligation that carries discomfort and privation. On the other hand, when you know that you are whole already, giving is sharing, and sharing enhances all feeling of self. The only thing sacrificed is the infantile notion of a sugar daddy in the sky who takes care of you no matter what. There is only one person whose job it is to take care of you, and that is yourself.

Discover your self, and you will know what being all-one is.

Relationships are life. Living as a human being in a human body is about learning to live, work, embody, manage, and embrace differences. We can only learn this by contemplating, confronting, resisting, and generally interacting with the very thing we wish to know, experiencing its complementary and opposing parts.

We exchange energy currents and form karmic bonds. Through the chords thus formed, we project and absorb different qualities. As we grow in consciousness and come to understand another and embrace each other with intelligent love, we ourselves adopt or absorb these characteristics. This is what understanding and compassion are all about.

As we attract whatever we are (in other words, what vibrates at the same frequency), energetic law compels us to relate to people who reflect our likes as well as our dislikes, until we contain and overcome these diversities in wholeness—that is to say, until we no longer feel attraction or repulsion. At this point, real love can begin. Not everyone understands this facet of relating, especially when sex is involved. Instinctual sex is predicated upon attraction or repulsion of bodies. Spiritual sex bases itself on soul attraction that irradiates the body when it is embraced in wholeness.

It is a matter of completion. Often, in the absence of a loved one or someone with whom we had an intimate relationship (which could also have been antagonistic), we feel as if he or she were inside us. We feel their characteristics expressing themselves through us as an emotion, a thought, or a gesture. We may find ourselves saying, "Oh, my God! I'm doing just what so-and-so used to do!" Or, "My goodness! This is what so-and-so must have felt when I did this to him!" Or we may simply feel their strength, reminding us that the experience with them has become an integral part of us now. Then we understand just how much we actually absorbed through the relationship. This happens mentally, emotionally, physically, and also spiritually. It is how we help one another, how we honor one another, how cellular memory extends through the body of humanity into the future.

When the whole becomes our own self, we not only understand all possible differences in genuine tolerance, we also realize that loneliness is an illusion. Now the companionship we sought is precisely what we are capable of offering, and the understanding we lacked comes forth as brotherhood in manifestation.

It is our active participation as women in the world that will make the real difference for the future of the race.

LETTER THIRTEEN: HOW IMPORTANT IS SEX?

My Empowering Love,

Much of today's sexuality is produced from the outside by props and mental imagery based on negotiable emotionality. It preys on insecurity and fear.

Sex, as an opening between worlds, is the place where the Mother weaves creation. It is an illogical, irrational gorge, a mysterious zone where life pours in, through, and out of form—the whirling, chaotic entrails of the source. The quality of consciousness determines the quality of the creations that issue forth. Those creations compose your future world.

Sex is fun, but too much of anything is harmful. The importance lies in quality of consciousness, in feeling-sensing* rather than in "doing." For the spiritual person, it is neither a pastime to be engaged in when there is nothing to do, nor is it something to be used over another. Neither is it a sport arena that provides an opportunity to measure performance skills and power. The point is what leads us to engage in sex, what gives it its power.

Now, men: I know it is not so fashionable these days to say this, but you need them, and they need you, *beyond sex*. This is not an emotional or mental need as much as a functional one, a creative collaboration. It is impossible to live out of one polarity alone. This is the divine trap that the Creator fashioned in order

---

feeling-sensing: The experience of both sensation and subtle emotion, or rather the rapport between them. Please note that sensations do not convey emotion; they are devoid of the emotional associations we create for and invest in them. So, whereas for some people sensation includes the quality of emotional feeling, for most people it may not.

to teach us co-creation and flexibility.

All relationships are essentially sexual because they deal with exchanges of energy substance at physical, mental, and emotional levels. The physical sexual relationship is the perfect arena for mutual empowering in the highest sense. But sex in the most common sense of the word is another matter; it is in the mind.

When the first stage of sexual desire is over, the intense attraction-and-repulsion cycle dwindles. Most people terminate the relationship then and there, and look for another who will kindle a state of constant physical excitement yet again, ignoring the mental and emotional consequences. This way, they never graduate into the subtleties of higher energetic correspondence that full relationships offer.

Male–female relating is a continuous play of vital and spiritual force. There is nothing to match or replace this kind of nourishment, except Nature itself. Sexual relationships with persons of the same gender generate peculiar exchanges at the mental and emotional levels. At the physical level, unless balanced in other ways, they produce tension and imbalance. Although often satisfactory for the more spiritually minded, they cannot attain the fullness at physical levels that the opposite polarity provides. Instead, they tend to create more craving. Relationships with the same sex can be healing, but they can also be energetically destructive when the physical aspect is not understood, balanced, and compensated for.

Ancient Tantrikas studied and devised compensational methods for people without partners or with partners of the same sex. They also devised methods for enhancing conscious energetic circulation between heterosexual couples to produce health and well-being. Drawing from the female power of generation, and combining it with masculine power of projection of consciousness, the sexual act was refined into a science of soul attainment. This is how we know that the physical human orgasm is but a small fraction of the orgasmic activity that occurs within trained initiates.

Orgasm is the very pulsation of life. It happens at many levels. Men cannot reach the deepest levels that women do. Female orgasm triggers an expanding orgasmic reflex that reverberates in wider and wider spheres of influence as creational processes.

The female orgasmic reflex, also produced by correspondences in nature and from higher emanations reached in meditation, first engulfs or enfolds a person, place, or activity, then spreads and progressively dilates into an endless rippling release. This pulsing activity affects and conditions *Aluna*—the state and substance of the female mind. The superior woman emits orgasmic orbs of exalted inspiration as joy and fulfilment all the time. Whereas a woman can produce this alone, man needs a woman to reach it. He needs the experience of being devoured by the Female Principle. This is what *Kali* represents.

It is not so much that sexual relating is necessary. It leads to the higher-frequency cellular emission, of which women are the custodians. For this reason, women have been the teachers and gurus of sexual practices throughout time. Rather than prostitution, priestesses conditioned cellular frequency for the uplifting of the race. Not all women are prepared to assume this responsibility. In truth, however, spirituality can be achieved directly for both men and women without sex.

Appreciate the difference and perfection of the sexes, my dearest one. See yourself within this immense universe of co-vibrating, interacting, and dancing parts. . .and evoke your divine origins. The Mother contains both male and female. It is in this sense that the origin of the race was said to be hermaphroditic or androgynous, a state that is entirely beyond our wildest imaginings.

LETTER FOURTEEN: WHY ARE MEN AFRAID OF ME?

My Deep, Dark Child,

One of the most perplexing things for us is how easily and lightly men seem to slip into and out of emotional love, how predictable they are to us, and how easily they are attracted to and entrapped by appearances. Everything is so very up-front.

Women are like a precipice. There is no way of reaching the secure cliff on the other side except by jumping over and past the intervening ravine. Yet how many people consciously welcome the experience of risk? Our strength and power comes precisely from the necessity of breaching a continuously irrational abyss.

There is not a man alive who has not been frightened of women at some level. Even Casanova found ways of courting danger and avoiding the loss of control. Men's instinctive fear of us provokes frustration and pain, to which we respond by implicit or explicit promises that pretend to justify our inner chaos. We complain about men's unfaithfulness and are confused by their apparent lack of correspondence with *our* feelings, but do we understand *ourselves?*

Men prize a certain kind of definition, one of form rather than content. They like routine and predictability. We don't normally consider these important, at least not for the same reasons as they do. They are naturally linear, rational creatures, less complicated. They are able to coolly oversee the emotional arena from their mental heights. As a direct result of our ability to move through and contain the irrational, we are the peace-producing agents of life. They, however, are the peace-sustaining vehicles for the mighty power that holds the world together.

Not all men are as obviously flitty as the flirt, or as shallow in feeling as the intellectual, but each in his own right harbors a fear of losing a part of himself. This part is the seed of the attraction towards his own completion as he learns to embrace the female as a *qualifying consciousness* within himself. Under ordinary circumstances, he will reflect your incompletedness and denial, or whatever is left of it, until such time as you recognize this and stand upon your strength of being and feeling. You, on the other hand, represent uncontrolled subconscious forces that are veiled within him.

When was the last time that you held a man in your arms—a lover, a brother, a friend, a little boy maybe. . .and witnessed his frailty? That is his need for the Mother through you, a need that he himself can't understand. And how often have you abused the circumstances, taking advantage of that need for your own purposes?

In your relationships with him, in friendship or in partnership, match his strength and power with your *own* kind—not in competition but in wholeness, as a separate, different, and equal child of God. Of course this requires valuing unqualified feeling in a world where concrete meaning is held in the highest esteem. This is precisely the point. It is why you as *you* are so necessary.

Man's fear of you mirrors your own. If you have confronted yourself, in your deep relating you will see, not fear, but reverence.

LETTER FIFTEEN: WHAT IS THE ATTRACTION
THAT I FEEL FOR WOMEN?

Dear Mysterious One,

Women have always been close to one another. Now we are denied that experience of intimacy in natural ways. For only another woman knows what a woman needs and feels. We can be a tremendous source of emotional and spiritual comfort and nourishment to one another.

Understand what attraction is and how it expresses itself in many ways. It manifests through bodies and polarities through a variety of means and on a number of levels. Sex is but one of them. Remove from your mind this automatic link you have created between attraction and sex, and try to see attraction, and its result, arousal, for what it is. We have forged such a habit of controlling and disconnecting from our bodies that we no longer understand arousal as a natural physical response. Instead, it is interpreted sexually.

Arousal is not necessarily sexual. It is a birdsong. It is joy in the flesh. It is our right to be full, excited, and happy for its own sake. We do not need to act on it or chase after the outside factors that stimulated it. As humans, and more specifically as human females, we need to distinguish between body chemistry and mental conditioning, and also between enjoyment and accomplishment. Attraction is absolutely neutral; arousal is a bodily state of being. What we choose to do with the experience, and the meaning we pour into it, fall into the category of life choices.

Observe what happens when two women are together. What do you feel that is different from what you feel when you are with men? What changes within you? Would you feel the same if you didn't know the gender of the forces at play? What are you responding to? At what level? Try to separate your perception of sensation from your emotions. Perceive the dynamic elicited by the presence of another person as an energy field. Perceive the sensations produced by any and all forms of life. If you remove the thought-process of sex from your mind, you are left with the experiencing of life directly.

Intimacy, and the need for it, although part of the greater picture, must not be confused with lovemaking and sex. It is time that society again accepts women being with women without projecting sexuality into it. Our nature is basically maternal and sensual, and to embrace, caress, kiss, touch hands, and care for another physically are absolutely natural expressions.

We must look upon this phenomenon, which is rapidly becoming fashionable, with the focused clarity and great urgency it requires. There is not only an obsession with time and spending, there is a tremendous amount of gender confusion creating unnecessary conflict, judgment, ostracism, and inner guilt. Once you let go of vested interests, collective fantasies, the pressure of attraction to darkly forbidden fruits, you find that your ideas about attraction, arousal, and sex are transformed. You become spontaneous.

My dearest one, will you allow yourself, not only to feel deeply, as is your nature, but also to *think* deeply? The call for blending with another is neither urgent nor accidental. Never be afraid to love. This includes demonstrations of love, caresses, hugs, soft kisses. . . . It is not the act, but the thinking process behind it, that lends it power and also sanctity. Dare to think. Dare to know. . . . Then your friendships, your alliances, relationships of every sort, including sexual, will express themselves very differently, and so will the forms through which you incite, excite, and stimulate your organism.

Love is Love, and many are its expressions. At its base is purity. Purity forever conveys serenity, wholeness, openness, and an overwhelming reverence for the holiness of all life.

LETTER SIXTEEN: HOW DOES THE EXPERIENCE OF SEX RELATE TO THE SOUL EXPERIENCE OF LOVE?

My Passionate One,

They meet in the experience of full release, the letting go of all references. And both are similar to the experience of death.

The love of the soul is neither of the pleasure of the body nor of the emotional satisfaction that women instinctively yearn for, yet it is constructed upon the experience of both. Rather it is both of these in progressively sublime levels of experience. This love is not fluffy or indiscriminate. Neither is it bossy, possessive, or manipulative. It is intense, but it does not derive from excess.

Let go of the fear as well as the attraction surrounding the loss of control associated with the pleasure of the body. As long as this persists, you are unable to experience any sort of love. Replace the darkness and isolation, which are a consequence of excess, with the awareness of life's abundance, in true innocence and purity.

The pleasure of the body is an index of health and vitality, flexibility and harmony. It includes the sense of touch but also the subtlest sensitivity evoked through spiritual awareness. This is the kind that leads to respect of the body, not to its exploitation. Emotional fulfilment echoes affinity and mutual responsiveness. It is centered in the present and in oneself, not in the other. Each party is whole.

The pleasure of spirit is intrinsically related to the presence of the divine as the individual connects with his or her source. When this happens during a partnership, each is individually attuned to his or her presence and does not demand from, or depend on, the other. We feel grateful, infinitely grateful, to the other who shares himself or herself with us in order to sustain the conditions that intensify the experience. There is absolutely nothing personal in this. And yet it is the greatest possible realization for both men and women. Its experience hums within the cells of the body and resonates through every feeling.

This love takes us into ecstatic surrender and conscious participation with life in a wider and wider circumference of joyfulness and creativity. It is a far cry from the poetic fantasy that colors the adolescent view of romance, for it is erected around individual responsibility, discernment, and the power of sustained harmony through all of life's conditions. Enlightened men and great women, like San Juan de la Cruz and Santa Teresa de Avila, are an eternal monument to this expression of love in the world. The presence of the other is never a distraction but a continual reminder of God's greatness.

Recognize the difference between each kind of pleasure. Look for beauty. Rescue the loveliness that lies at the heart of every form, every action, every feeling.

You are the qualifying agent of the precious force of love in *all* its manifestations. Practice selectiveness, not denial. There is nothing to run away from or anywhere to run to. There is nothing to resist or exclude. Life is always *here,* and it is beautiful. The darkness through which you may pass always contains light. Know this as you journey through the depths of life and your own self.

Letter Seventeen: Can I Be "Pure" and Still Lead a Full Life?

Beloved Priestess of My Light,

Daughter of my own heart, both purity and power are yours. I see you as the scintillating stillness that reflects the bottom of a rich, silent pool; you dive deeply but also reflect on the surface the currents of love as they seek to express themselves within the entrails of the world, sometimes purely, sometimes not.

Do not confuse purity with naïveté. Because you feel others' feelings, you think that they also feel them. Not so! And when you sense their distress, you naturally wish to spare them. Alas! Understand the deceitful surface of feelings, and concentrate on the *faculty* that allows you to feel. It will let you truly see. Knowing is enough. You do not need to prove it or have it proven to you. You do not need to act.

Do not confuse purity with repression. Sometimes, if distress is high, you justify whatever will shield you from that intensity. This can also apply to body sensations. There is no way you can short-circuit the human experience of feeling. It would be tantamount to stopping a tsunami. You are its unqualified gauge. Confusion sets in only when you are outside yourself. Then you can't tell right from wrong and are inclined to believe anything. You become gullible and silly. You do not *need* to do anything.

Do not, moreover, confuse purity with puritanical behavior. At your core is innocence. This innocence is not stupidity, childishness, or life-denying prudishness. It is the quality of your feeling when it is devoid of qualification and reveals the potent pool of wisdom that is purity. Know it to be the fountain in which feelings are born and to which they return and are contained in temperance and maturity. When, however, you allow this power of the heart to be handled and managed by the analytical mind, you become ruthlessly shrewd. It is this characteristic that separates the priestess from the witch. Simply feel and watch.

Woman is the doorway through which feelings enter into humanity. Perhaps for this reason we have been typecast as seductresses. You are seen as the perennial Eve who tempts man with the forbidden fruit, which of course you do, as knowledge that is both transcendent and primary. We *are* the serpent's breath. But the Holy Spirit is the One who breathes within us. We are both innocence and wisdom.

The way of woman dictates that we reach illumination through the depths and heights of felt intuition. This is symbolized both by the serpent as by the dove. Consciousness is attained through Being, when the flight of the serpent as a dove is serenely perched beyond the ebb and flow of movement itself and becomes Quetzalcoatl, the Christ force.

Our intelligence operates on a knowing which is a not-knowing. If we can somehow grasp this state as pure experience. . .if we can hold that moment and extend it out through and beyond time. . .we return to the state of the priestess, our original role in the temples of God's grace.

The return of the priestess state requires that woman hold the silence. In the stillness of her awareness, as Consciousness, the pool of felt substance that flows from the female mind gathers into a fathomless well of wisdom and primeval matter. Priestesses were taught how to sustain the silence of being female. From this sourcing presence, priests were able to access substance, and the faculty with which to do their work as fashioners of form and measure, as well as makers and keepers of knowledge.

It isn't easy to embrace the serpent in innocence. Time and again, we fall victims to suggestion, the tool of the sinister force as subconscious human influence. Its outer manifestations are gossip, social pressure to conform, worry, suspicion, and the perpetual preoccupation with what others will say or think. It is corrosive and sinks its tentacles even more deeply than the corresponding doubt that clouds the minds of men. It numbs our sensitivity and deflects intuition. Know how to recognize suggestion.

Purity is the greatest of all powers in this world and the source of all other real power. The purity I speak of now is the one reached through the full experience of life. Peel yourself away from the convincing profusion of images that crowd your mind for attention, the fascinating emotions that entice you into turbulent intensity. Retain this silence as you resist the onslaught of pictures and emotions bombarding the frequencies of substance. These are the elemental subconscious creations of humanity with which you ally yourself, unless you choose to stand on your own.

LETTER EIGHTEEN: HOW TO ACCESS AND EMPLOY POWER IN THE WORLD WHEN IN TRUTH I FEEL VULNERABLE AND UNSURE?

Sweet Yielding One,

However it manifests, power is the strength to stand whole and alone. It does not imply pressure or the aggressive force demanded in your world today.

Your nature is in softness. But that softness is also yieldingness. It is extremely strong precisely because it can bend. In the suppleness, it gathers momentum. Know the ways of the willow tree bending with the wind, the power of being vulnerable. In that flexibility is the ability to receive, and be impregnated by, myriad forces and qualities. This must not be confused with fragility, which is an appearance. Just as the flower is fragile in its momentary existence, so does it reproduce and spread and persist throughout time, in its own timing, always itself.

The forces you handle and contain condition, qualify, and stabilize the world. They are in your body but not of it. They are in your feelings, but not your feelings. They are in your mind, but are not your thoughts. They represent the womb of the earth, your receptivity to humanity, to all your children. They are present as the ability for peace and the enormous resilience that experiencing various postures simultaneously can give you.

You are so strong, my beloved daughter—so much so that you protect the children of the world, all of them, including the men! The Father counts on this. He counts on you and me.

Be as soft and as vulnerable as you are, but do so with dignity. You will always feel unsure because security is an illusion.

LETTER NINETEEN: SPEAK TO ME
OF THE FEMALE WARRIOR.

My Tenacious One,

All my daughters are warriors of the fiercest kind. Know that the female warrior trains her body and also her mind. She is a master of *Aluna*. She fights the earthly with the earthly, yet her consciousness is forever perched upon the altar of the Law. As the Hindu Kali, you are the Mother's cyclical expression, in essential attunement with Her as nature. You have been consecrated.

Understand: Fighting is not against your nature. It is the very expression of your love and essential righteousness. Yours is the courage and strength of the heart. But don't degrade yourself fighting over trivial things. Especially, don't respond to aggression aggressively, because you will be sure to lose.

The ways of Love obey the finer frequencies of higher Law. Your ammunition is more powerful than the one conveyed through brute force alone. When no other means are appropriate, you are allowed to use physical means—and then they are never your own. We become the vehicle of divine Justice, the all-powerful *Maat* of Egyptian lore.

When we are moved by the spirit of Truth, we are unbeatable. This truth is that of motherhood that engenders affinity with all of life—mineral and plant as well. We could say that woman is a warrior of the Light. There is nothing airy-fairy about this.

All of Life's resources obey woman's command in the heavens as upon the Earth—from within the very womb of creation. When life calls its children upon the Earth, it must do it as the Mother. When it clothes them, it must do so through the texture of the Mother's body. It is obliged to employ the Mother's feeling nature and to hold all in her heart.

You are my holy messenger and my own vehicle upon the Earth.

Letter Twenty: What Is Our Role In This World, In This Time?

My Own, the Woman of the Future,

Just as your breadth is wide and your depth is fathomless, so great too is your responsibility to prepare the way for the children of the future. It is in your hands. Men need you, and children are already waiting for you. Your action is imminently necessary. The world will not change until you change yourself first.

Everything that pertains to life and the rivering course of living belongs to you. If our men are to lead the world and illumine it with the light of the Father expressed through them, they are to do this on the ground which you prepare and which you hold for them. You are the sustaining power of truth in the world.

There is much that you can do silently, invisibly—your loving has never needed any other meaning than itself. But there is also much that you can do *visibly* in the world. Your dynamic and inspired leadership includes conveying and therefore teaching sensitivity in all its ways. This is why education is your privileged and primary stage, as it has always been in the home.

With healthcare, too, you can transmit tenderness, appreciation, and respect for the human body and its perfection. There is nothing like your physical touch and your emotional embrace to awaken healing forces. And as in medicine, so too in all the sciences, you can be an instrument for greater awareness of life's subtleties. These often go unnoticed. They are ever important in the dynamic of the intelligence of the heart, the intelligence within and through all of life.

There is no one like you to incorporate fairness and equality everywhere. This includes jurisdiction and government. You may not crave center stage, but you are an ever necessary pillar for the temple of God's Law through politics as through finance. Real economy, and the correct use of resources, are a natural consequence of your gratitude for living things.

Finally, your lovely sinuous form upon the earth is, and has always been, an object of admiration and veneration. Through it, and beyond it, you are capable of elevating the sensitivity of sensation into the aesthetic proportions of spirituality and transcendence. You preserve within your heart the real and eternal values of humankind. It is time you knew and lived this. . .all of it.

You will instinctively and consciously point all to the true priorities for humanity, the beloved children of your heart. Don't lie back and let another do what only you can do. As it did for Joan of Arc, the power of celestial might will always clear the way before you when you command in the name of Love.

Part Two

Training
And Development

THE ASKING

MOTHER!

How can I give form to myself,
and be and say, and touch
all of your children on this earth,
when I still feel an infant in your fold?
Show me how to transform myself
into the celestial-human creature
of your dreaming Mind.
Guide each step I take
and
teach me now. . .
to be upon the ground
that which I am within you
in Eternity!

THE TRANSFERENCE

DAUGHTER!

Take my hand and,
little by little, begin this day
to shape the matter of your self,
patiently, carefully, deliberately. . .
one small aspect at a time.
Use your mind, which is my Light;
exercise your feelings, which are
the very fiber of my soul;
and wear your body as the noble vestment it is,
the form that I must use.
And build, my sweetest one,
my temple of purity once again
within this ancient holy realm.

PREPARING FOR
THE FEMALE INITIATION

WOMEN ABSORB AND TRANSFORM. Our function involves simultaneously embracing and distancing. However subtly, Consciousness, through our gender, always seeks to lift us to the height and amplitude of clarity and serenity. As an archetype, it befalls heavenly Durga, or Mother Mary, through Isis and Ishwari, manifesting in work that requires giving of ourselves without identifying with what we see, feel, or do in a personally possessive way.

For the right to be a real woman and participate in the scheme of spiritual hierarchy as conscious, dependable collaborators in the world, we are tried and tested in daily tasks until our conscious awareness includes the use of all three bodies—physical, emotional, and mental—as a unit. This is the process of initiation. In women it calls for different skills than it does in men.

Before we can embrace both light and dark, good and evil, we collapse repeatedly, spending a good deal of the time in a moody underworld, as we do in the cyclical hypersensitivity surrounding menstruation. When we tire of being victims to our own lower selves, we tap into the riches of our intelligent, discerning intuition, which consists neither of will power nor aggression. This is not so easy. The desire to be who we really are becomes our guiding light as life persistently puts us through hardships. Potential must match life demands flexibly and powerfully as we learn to use and sustain Consciousness.

This is no ordinary testing. We never really know if we pass until we are well beyond the experience. Success implies transcendence, a versatility, and an ability to sustain extremely high levels of intensity. Whereas for men initiation concerns physical and mental abilities, for women it involves emotional introspection and spiritual fortitude—the courage, that is, to be and use both light and dark energies with purity. The correct responses equate with the ability to meet unexpected and energetically powerful emotional situations with tranquillity and with spiritual rather than emotional force. We are tried in the most absurd, irritating, and sometimes violent circumstances, depending upon our temperament. Our conception of love and spirituality is reformulated many, many times.

We prepare for this testing of the self by the Self for our entire life—for many lives, actually. This second part contains exercises to help us become who and what we are and better equip us, as Consciousness, for our tasks within the world. The training sketches contained in this section are merely suggestions, to be expanded by you in your world. Each exercise points to an aspect of our expression as physical, emotional, or mental energy, teaching us discernment and focus. Each woman should create her own exercises to suit her needs and pace, parting from the examples given and from the introspective abilities gained herewith.

For the more difficult unravelling of the deep subconscious influences of the psyche that dominate our gender, it will be necessary to rescue the forces invested with selfish and sinister qualifications from within the personality, and to learn to use emotional power with the mastery of Light. Both the second and third parts of this book may help here.

When we feel ready to embrace the darkness contained within the egoism of our own human personality, our very incompleteness confronts us through many circumstances. We begin—some of us slowly, others impetuously—to tread the path of apprenticeship and initiation. At this point, armed with the vehicles of our own consciousness, we set out into the very womb of darkness. The fierceness we thus encounter, no matter how many times we believe it is unbearable, never exceeds what we can bear, because it is our own energy returning home. It is humanity calling within our very selves.

The scenario varies with the individual and the level of consciousness being tested. For each woman, it is a uniquely different saga. We may be tried for patience if impulsiveness has been the pattern of our egoism. We may need to learn yieldingness and acceptance if we have been rigid and stubborn, or trust if we have been exceedingly independent. It may even be spontaneity with which we are challenged, if we've tended to be calculating, physical expression if we have repressed it. . .or any combination of all these. Circumstances consist of minor encounters so commonplace that we would hardly notice them until they arise to cause a major battle.

It doesn't matter whether we *know* something if we are not able to *live* it. The knowing has to be incorporated and then sustained. This last skill is especially difficult, as it requires enormous flexibility learned under the most improbable conditions. In each changing gestalt, we learn to discriminate, choose decisively, and act impeccably. We recognize time and time again the hand of God at work in and through Creation, through darkness and into the light that casts no shadow because it embraces all. When we can distinguish truth from falsity—God's countenance *here* in every moment, regardless of appearances—we have come home, and the testing ends. . .for the moment.

EXERCISES

The exercises suggested below require concentration and application. At first they may not be easy. They call for creating discipline and evoking willingness to perceive in ways other than we usually do. They require we forget who we thought we were and discover ourselves anew.

1. The Sacred Female Form

When you bathe, or shortly thereafter, take the time to touch and feel your body. You may begin simply by looking at, and touching, a foot, a hand. . . .

Never mind the judgments you may have had about it. Notice its shape and textures. Remind yourself that it is the Mother's form, and that holy spiritual forces are at work there. Appreciate them and each body part you contemplate.

Now, as you touch it, become aware of feeling that touch at the skin level. Marvel at the perfection and the intricacy of this creation. Now pass into the inside of it and feel it *being* touched.

Bless that foot, that hand. . .each and every part of your body. "Blessing" means loving it and appreciating it for its service to you, for its beauty and its perfection. This may also trigger a train of thought concerning just how each part of your body serves you and what it means to the whole.

You are perceiving your body through the eyes of a mother, in the light of love's perfection. Witness the power of that love to inspire, transform, and exalt the object of its affection.

Sense what that blessing produces in your foot and in each part of your body.

Proceed to bless the whole body. Become aware that the

Mother feels what you feel. Everything you touch. . .each thing that you do. . .is the Mother's activity upon the Earth.

Appreciate the great privilege of incarnating the sacred female form.

2. *Quality Beyond Form*

The main purpose of this exercise is to distinguish appearance from content, so that, ultimately, you may be able to integrate them harmoniously in your own self.

Feel yourself. Do this in the way that comes most naturally. Simply feel what you feel to be feeling yourself.

Notice whatever props you may be tempted to use to define yourself—such as another's image of you, special circumstances, looking into the mirror. . .and try *not* to use them. Just be you as you. Write down your feelings.

Now think about who you are. This means extending your feeling to include the way you *think* that you are, and also what you are not. Define yourself.

Consider what others say that you are, or are not. What you think you should be or say you should be. . . . Make a list of these considerations and opinions.

Now stop. Just look at your image in the mirror as if you were looking at it for the very first time, impartially.

Examine the quality beyond the form you are now viewing. Sense the feelings within.

Put the thoughts, feelings, and images together. What are you?

Are you the same on the inside as you appear on the outside? Or rather, do you express or appear one quality while feeling another?

Play with these different ingredients until you can see in the mirror what you feel within, in the absence of any of the labels. Be one—inside and outside.

3. *Beyond Duality, Into Unity*

Conceive of polar feelings, like those you encounter in your everyday world.

Become aware of how you can swing from gullibility and naïveté to shrewdness and suspicion.

Observe the attractions and repulsions. . .the love—hate mixture of feelings for your loved ones. . .the dark—light situations of joy and fear combined. . .danger—security. . . abundance—lack . . .excitement—boredom. . . .

Make a list of those experiences that form part of your life.

Make another list of those that are *not* part of your life but that you have perceived as being part of *others'* experience.

Explore each possibility by remembering and observing your feelings at one extreme, then at the other.

Now, instead of resting on the emotional and physical aspect, shift to being a knowing Being consciously acknowledging the power of the God's source or presence.

Allow your spontaneous feeling to provide the experience of unity for you. Notice how this is neither thought nor emotion, although you will be aware of both.

Neither is it physical sensation. It embraces all.

Practice this shifting of a sense of your position as a basic requisite for all the other exercises and meditations.

Be a part, be all. . . . Be a part, be all. . . . Go into . . .and *out* of, *identification* with the various sensations of your body, your feelings, your thoughts, as you allow your experience of the ups and downs of everyday life but remain unswayed by either.

4. *Grounding And Centering*

Empty your mind and feel yourself experiencing the moment purely as emptiness within your body.

Your body feels sensations, but they appear as something separate from who or what you are. You have the choice of acquiring the properties of whatever you choose. The moment you identify with something, you take on its qualities.

Consider what you might be like without the physical form to anchor you, and contain the sensations, memories, and impressions that surround you.

Now choose to identify with the matter of your body consciously.

Sense your skin as the texture of the Earth and your body as its density.

Notice the sense of security and solidity this brings you. The Consciousness of the Earth is your grounding. You accentuate sensation at the same time as you inhabit your body more fully.

Practice alternately distancing yourself from, and fusing with, the sensations. They are associated with matter and the body of the Earth. Instead, you are the intelligence energizing this form.

Time doesn't exist here. There is only the present, a sensation of vastness that is also expansive. There is no hurry. No doing.

You contain all of time and also all its parts. You are the finished act and also the readiness to act.

Sensations of feeling come and go. Watch them swell and sink, and fresh ones emerge. . . . Allow their ripples to pass by you, their sonic imprints to ebb and flow beyond your form.

Expand your body to spread and fuse with the Earth. Feel how you are not alone. You are strong, changing yet immortal. Imperishable.

Become aware of the center from which you observe. This should be a definite physical location. If it isn't, and you sense yourself apart from the body, reposition yourself until you make both your emotional and your sensation centers coincide.

You are a wholeness within a part. This part is also whole.

5. Levels Of Reality In The World

The effects produced by your physical, emotional, and mental presence in the world are great. In this exercise you will perceive how your environment affects you while you also affect it. Observe yourself in your ordinary surroundings, physically, emotionally, and mentally.

A. PHYSICAL REALITY

Review a typical day. Decide to be as neutral as you can.

Remember a day just the way you lived it, from inside yourself looking out.

Observe others being affected by your physical presence and your actions. Take the time now to notice what you may not have noticed at the time.

You may perceive waves of feeling and sense undulations that return to you from others. To some, you will be giving vitality; from others, you will be attracting it.

Be centered only on what *you* are feeling and sensing.

Some people may contract around you. This is not the moment to analyze the phenomenon. Just take note.

Notice your own shifts.

Your body compels definition. Just what is your physical impact on others this day?

What do you think, or feel, that they see and expect from you?

Now, observe yourself in your physical world again, but this time do it from outside your body looking in, as if you were watching yourself in a film.

What do you see now? What do you feel now?

If there is any judgment coming in, go over the exercise again and again until you can witness yourself and your world as a configuration of ebbs and flows and qualities of movement.

B. EMOTIONAL REALITY

It is fundamental that you distinguish between the sensations of the body and the spiralling, wavering activity of the emotions.

Define the overall emotional atmosphere that you breathe when you are by yourself, in your own energy.

Now observe the changes in that quality when you are thinking about someone or something.

Observe the changes in your emotional quality when you contact the tangible reality of the outer world in your daily life.

Feel what happens the moment a desire or memory slips in.

In specific situations you choose, notice your expressions, veiled or manifest.

How many of those you perceive relate directly to you?

Which originate with you?

Which are you amplifying?

Which are you projecting—i.e., imagining—onto someone else?

Where do feelings come from?

What do you do with them?

Where do they go?

Which feelings do you prefer?

What would you be like without these feelings?

As you did with physical observation, follow this up with perception at a distance.

Observe the actual power of your emotional force.

Balance yourself with physical grounding now.

C. MENTAL REALITY

Establish the neutral environment of your mind at peace. Distinguish this from the physical sensation of your body and the emotional experience of yourself.

Contrast the feeling produced by your mind when it is at peace with that produced when you are worried. Choose a non-emotional "worry," such as a problem involving math or the like.

Make a list of your common worries. List them all in order of importance. Notice the charge produced by each one separately, and how some of them feed others.

How many of them were fed by the emotions?

Look at the *quality* of your thoughts. Which are more meaningful?

Are these the kinds of thoughts that you want to have? Distinguish between the comfortable and the uncomfortable ones.

Now observe yourself in your daily contact with others, in your conversations and evaluations. Pick one specific moment.

What do you say? What do you think but *not* say?

Notice others' reactions to your words. . .and thoughts.

Distinguish the different origin of your thoughts. These are basically three:

- your own
- those that come from other people
- those obligations, superstitions, or phobias that come from social or cultural expectations and beliefs ingrained within you

Notice how many thoughts you believed were yours were *actually* yours.

6. Environmental Resonance

In the earlier context, you distinguished among physical, mental, and emotional expression. It is important that you do this now vibrationally, noticing different frequencies and how energies play through, and upon, your body.

Behavior patterns respond to energetic configurations. If you learn how this operates, you can more effectively understand and correct your responses to life's situations.

You may sense each relationship as a sound, reverberation, or oscillation in your body and its surrounding energy field. Sometimes these perturbations will affect one area more than another. At others, you will feel them in your whole body. There will be moments when you perceive them outside, or around, the physical body. Sharpen your awareness of this phenomenon.

Contrast your experience of different environments and surroundings, one at a time. Feel yourself feeling, and in this sense *relating* with, trees, plants, rivers, streams, the earth. . . .

The harmonies are different in each case.

Perceive where there is dissonance or discord. What in your energy produces that sensation? How can you neutralize it?

Observe yourself with other human beings. Their resonance is different, more variable, and more complex than those of environments. Don't blend with them; simply feel the interplay of forces.

Begin with children.

Then continue with friends, both male and female.

Proceed to your usual work space, a supermarket, the hairdresser's, a night club, your home, a church. . .etc.

Which places, and sorts of people, make you buzz?

Which places and people slacken or deplete your energy?

Discover why, and how, these specific energies add to, or subtract from, your own.

Carefully examine each of your sensations and feelings separately, studying them as if they were objective data.

Distinguish among harmonious, discordant, vital physical, emotional, intellectual, friendly, convenient, comfortable, peaceful, thrilling, aggressive, and serene relating.

Finally, decide which elements, ingredients, and qualities you wish to fill your world.

7. Likes And Dislikes

Make a list of your likes, in order of preference. Study the motivations behind them. This means asking yourself why you like them and how they serve you.

Do the same with your dislikes. Ask how they create disturbance or inconvenience for you.

See each kind of attraction and repulsion for what it is: an energetic happening conditioned by belief, habit, or some signal originating somewhere else. Stay as neutral as you can.

Now experiment with the reversal of your attitudes. Actually change your feelings.

Compare both experiences.

Check and balance your feelings henceforth. You will find that you soften the categorization of experience considerably.

8. The Power Of Qualification

This exercise is especially valuable in learning to control the emotional body, in learning to distance oneself at will without cutting off from feeling.

Evoke the physical demeanor, emotional expressions, turn of mind, and likes and dislikes of a loved one. . .the tastes, and especially what he or she triggers in you. The way you feel around, about, or without him or her. . . .

Remember how you miss him, or her, when they're not around, and how you also feel relieved when they are gone and you have time and space for yourself. . . .

Keep focusing on the way that you *feel*. . . . Recognize this feeling, *your* feeling.

Now, distance yourself from your feeling. Notice its quality.

Go in and come out of this feeling at will.

Become aware of any associations that this feeling may have. In other words, does it remind you of someone or some other thing? Does it evoke a situation, real or imaginary?

Repeat the observation of your loved one, but, this time, as if it concerned a total stranger.

What links you to your relationships is your qualification, a feeling of personal gratification that brings meaning to you.

9. *Discerning And Appreciating*

Watch people. Observe strangers as they pass by.

Distinguish what you consider their assets from their limitations. Even if you think you are making it up, give yourself permission to know this. This is not analysis but rather an exercising of your intuition.

Follow your hunches playfully, paying just enough attention to them that they don't go away, but not too much that you believe them.

Can you tell when someone is being genuine, spontaneous, at ease within himself? How is it that you know this?

Can you pick up on someone who appears phony, tense, ill-at-ease, pretentious? What leads you to spot that?

Now, focus on finding people's inherent good qualities, what is *real* in them. How do you do this?

Now, for no reason at all, appreciate each for who they are and the experience they offer you to discover your self.

10. *Wanting And Having*

People want things. They want a relationship. They want a child. . .often for the wrong reasons: to feel complete, to find a purpose. As you think about either of these desires, take note of your reasoning. If your desire is different from either of these, adapt the following process accordingly.

Involve yourself in the future fantasy of going through courtship, romance, and partnership. . .or conception, pregnancy, and birth *(or any other particular desire of your own).*

Follow this through. Make it real. What will people think and say? What and how do you *feel* about what they think and say?

Now, examine your motivation. Is it something you feel you *need*? In this case, feel the urgency and self-centeredness.

Is it something you would dearly like? In this case, feel how important and necessary it is that you have a relationship, a child, by a certain age. . .and so on.

Is it, on the other hand, motivated by something else—abundance within you to share and give, an overflow you can sense that is neither urgent nor problematic? You would know right timing and right action instinctively.

If you were turned off by the whole exercise, look again at the degree of refusal involved in ordinary wants, especially those involving sharing and intimacy.

Try this with your career projections, your place in the world, your group affiliations.

Closely inspect those motivations and their surrounding feeling imagery. Understand how you actually fashion them—and, most importantly, the quality of your feeling behind your behavior.

Take note how you have exactly what you want. As a whole-body being-and-feeling state, observe how you bring this about automatically.

Do you reach for it, thus expanding and stirring conditions in your environment?

Or do you retreat and attract, somehow contracting and drawing towards you?

When do you go from one to the other form of having?

Lastly, and most importantly, can you *release* what you bind to yourself?

Can you allow yourself to receive without wanting?

11. *Friendship: Embracing And Requalifying*

Evoke the love you feel for a very dear friend. Feel the quality rather than the object of your feeling. Enjoy loving for loving's sake.

Consider how real friendship, like brotherhood or sisterhood, manifests concretely in your life circumstances.

Think about how you love someone even when they do not love themselves, how you are there for them through their mistakes and confusions.

Consider the return for this love. Do you allow it in? Do you allow the person to be there for you through *your* mistakes and confusion?

Center once again on the feeling of loving for love's sake. Cultivate that feeling. Reproduce it at will.

Practice feeling accepted and cherished—until it becomes the atmosphere that you breathe.

Practice loving everyone because you enjoy it, and feel your own wholeness embracing you.

Thank your beloved friend for teaching you the meaning and feeling of love in its highest human expression.

12. *Feeling Flexibility*

Sensation is very different from emotion. Mind itself produces neither sensation nor emotion, yet it fuels both to the point where a sensation, an emotion, and a thought become indistinguishable.

Your thoughts determine the quality of your feelings, but your emotions color your thoughts. Observe how you are locked inside this vicious circle. Especially notice the repetitive thinking pattern behind obsessive behavior. Whereas an emotion—a feeling, that is—may find justification in a thought, the thought holds and binds the feeling in a form.

Choose a typical obsessive thought with the purpose of studying it.

Separate the feeling from its accompanying thought. You do this by focusing only on the feeling as a sensation. As you center yourself in it without labels, you are able to contain the movement of the feeling.

Stay with it until you are certain you can sustain it impartially.

By the quality of the expanding waves you sense, you will know when you are beyond the thoughts that feed and bind the emotion.

Now you may change the quality of the thoughts appropriately.

You do this by determining the level from which you are feeling. Is this feeling connected to physical sensation? Where? How?

What produces it? Does it come from outside you, or is it issuing from your personal emotional world?

Examine the automatic responses involved.

Now *choose* what you want to feel, and the thoughts you want to have.

You can think clearly only when you are in *the right feeling state.* Otherwise you elude and manipulate yourself and others. Practice producing the right feeling state, until you can do it instantly.

13. Empathy And The Pool Of Experience

Pay close attention to the context of memories having to do with certain people. Think of someone, and then feel the *quality* of the memory he or she evokes in you. Each person will bring a unique quality, even if the experiences you shared with them appear similar.

Do this with several different people. Some people give off a certain joy; others are simply depressing; some have a bitter-sweet feel to them; yet others may exude serenity and cool. Be sure you base yourself on your *feeling* of them and not on mental *conclusions* about them.

Allow yourself to take in each quality impersonally, even if it is very different from what you would prefer to have.

Thank each person for having touched your life, and for giving you this precious memory substance that you may now use.

Become aware of how these experiences and their qualities become a part of you, as understanding, in empathy and sympathy. *(These will include mother, father, friends, enemies, teachers. . .even places, animals, and things.)*

See how you use them now and how you could best use them in the future.

We don't actually need to personally explore all experience directly, if we can attune to that of others who have gone before us. We can learn much from the collective pool of experience.

You will be surprised how you come to *know* simply by *wanting* to know.

14. Orgasmic Reflex And Co-Creation

Once you have differentiated varieties of resonance and energy exchanges from a distance, invisibly, observe yourself with some-one of the opposite sex whose energy vitalizes yours.

Focus upon the orgasmic reflex. This is to say the physical sensation produced, emotional feelings evoked, and mental interest stirred.

Don't *create* what you wish to see or feel. Simply observe each kind of pulsation for tone, quality, variability, and versatility.

Notice the particular orchestration you produce, allowing it to deepen and rise in its own way.

Now, if you already have a sexual partner, explore further. Become aware of your own activity at the different levels as you share in the sexual experience. Observe him or her, yourself, and the energy field you create together.

Take note of the thought forms you co-create jointly and release out into the world about you through physical, mental, or emotional intercourse, professional affiliation, or other co-creational projects.

15. Exchanging Perspectives

Men and women are teachers for one another.

Ask your male partner *(lacking this, a male friend)*, to share with you the ways in which he perceives life.

Let him see the way you see him. *(It is a big shift from trying to make him fit your mold, or adapting yourself to what you think are his expectations.)*

Now ask his permission to enter his energy field. You will do the same for him.

Notice the different forces at play, how you feel, move, think, act. . . . Consider how body shape and polarities condition your behavior.

Open to the experience of the other beyond words.

As you sense a person at their core, as they themselves perceive reality, you will find a place for each one in your fathomless heart.

16. Having Vs. Giving

Imagine a situation in which you feel contented and fulfilled. You have everything: physical comfort, emotional and material security, pleasure at every level, and prestige.

Give yourself permission to indulge in the feeling of having all this and the safety it brings. Relish it for as long as you like.

Now step aside from the feeling and sensation of having. Return to neutrality and serenity.

Imagine someone else in your place. Choose a specific person, and see *them* now enjoying the very same things that you gave yourself.

Imagine consciously giving a second, and then a third person your place, your space. . .and enjoying seeing her or him delight in all that, just as you did!

Contrast the feeling you had of enjoyment for yourself with the feeling of enjoying your experience of someone else's enjoyment.

17. Responsiveness Vs. Excitation

Observe your sexual feelings and sensations to study what triggers them. Notice whatever props, imagery, or feelings you require for sexual stimulation and satisfaction.

Separate thoughts, feelings, and sensations to reveal which aspects predominate.

Distinguish between what *happens* spontaneously and what you *do* to intensify an experience or produce an effect.

Now *contrast* this with those sensations and subtle movements you detect while alone in a natural setting.

Close your eyes and allow the rhythms of nature to stir you. Allow yourself to participate as *responsiveness*.

Permit the energy to pool within you.

Simply appreciate the pleasure of living life in your whole body.

Notice the quality of your energy and the enormous array of open possibilities.

Explore your relationship with energies within and around you.

18. Becoming A Cup

This exercise has been conceived for heterosexual partners but may be adapted for any circumstances involving loving relations between people.

When there is love, there is almost nothing that you will not do to make another happy and to honor them for the love they evoke in you.

Begin with prayer. Become aware of your heart, and allow it to expand and embrace your partner as your arms embrace them. Become a cup from which they may drink your love.

Evoke their loveliness, all those things you treasure.

Mentally link your vagina with your heart. Most of the time you will feel them instantly and spontaneously connected.

Allow the light you sense in your heart to flow, from the tip of your breasts towards their heart.

As you become softer and softer, more malleable, blend with them.

Offer them the whole of your body. In other words, your entire form is involved and fuses with them.

Bring godliness into it! Lovemaking is a prayer of gratitude to God for life, for Being, for having such a wonderful companion with whom to share it.

The two of you become a rivering whole.

As they empty themselves within you, you empty yourself into their heart.

Visualize your bodies enveloped within a mantle of Light.

If you can do this consciously together, you may offer yourselves as a unit to God, visualizing yourselves within an iridescent globe of peace.

Pray that your energies be used towards the healing of the whole. Know that angelic presences will see to this.

End with grateful prayerfulness.

19. *Balancing Dark And Light: Integration*

Recapitulate the sequence of events during trying times in your life, and study your reactions. See what life was trying to teach you, how much of it you learned, and how much you have yet to develop.

For a period of time each night, review your reaction to unexpected events. Change the way you react automatically, and place a conscious response in its stead. You will need to adjust feelings to thoughts, and thoughts to feelings.

Try to live those new ways, carefully acknowledging the areas that need work. Work a little at a time, changing aspects rather than whole behavioral patterns.

Use introspection, and gradually transfer your intended behavior patterns onto your physical activity.

When faced with an old impulse. . .*hold* it. Harness that energy. Notice what happens. Conceive instead of what *could* happen if you direct the energy differently.

Alternatively, step aside from an emotionally turbulent situation. Offer, elevate, or otherwise replace your reaction with a conscious intention.

Instead of allowing feelings of guilt or self-recrimination, or giving free vent to your passions, embrace both the light and the dark within yourself.

Without diminishing your energy, move *the quality* of the energy you would otherwise repress, condemn, or indulge in. In other words, use the strength of anger, the expanded awareness of fear, or the potent force of passion as a wholly neutral force.

Treat the embracing expansiveness of felt intelligence as a *thing*, that is, without disassociating it from the concrete world.

As you seek to balance light and dark in your everyday activities, it is important under all circumstances to not freeze the flow of energy.

Only the courage to be and willingness to act can liberate the fullness of that which you are.

20. Motherhood

If, for some reason you are unable, or do not wish, to have children, the following exercise can be highly gratifying personally as it liberates useful thought forms into the world.

In everything but the physical reproduction aspect, the experience of gestation and birthing is very similar to that of lovemaking, co-creating, and idealization.

Physical motherhood gives us the privilege of exploring the materialization of the female heart's desires. This experience marks the realization for women at the physical level and combines all possible forms of relating with the elements and qualities of Nature.

Become aware of your maternal instincts in relation to life and the world. Every woman has them: Identify how *yours* express themselves.

Be careful not to impose cultural descriptions, but rather discover the ways in which you naturally respond to living processes, in which you seek to embrace, heal, inspire, and preserve the delicate sanctity of life in all its different areas: with people, children, animals, plants, mineral life. . .in ecology, politics, education. . . .

Intensify your feelings until you envelop the person, place, or thing. And expand and deepen that instinct until you allow all possible feelings within yourself.

Notice what you feel moved to do.

Elaborate the fantasy as you quicken and augment those natural impulses. See how far it takes you into that which your heart desires in the broadest ways.

Then pause.

Use the natural intelligence of the heart to discover what you *can* do.

Reconsider how you can actually improve the world today.

Now do it.

21. *Protection And Healing Creations*

Do not confuse caring and caretaking—both of which project your own substance into form—with worrying over something or someone. This latter behavior is filled with fear and tension and gives birth to forms that are physically bound to the subject.

You protect and heal life forms all the time. Observe just how.

See what you do to defend, protect, or inspire someone. Observe your thoughts and the quality of your feelings.

Resist the fears and limitations of your personality that might seduce you into energizing weakness.

Now conceive of ways to protect and heal.

Give yourself all the time you need to carefully formulate a thought form. Empower it with the highest-quality feeling.

Focus or condense the thought and the feeling in your heart. Rather than being emotional, notice that this is pure intelligence.

In order to adapt it to the needs of the third dimension, you will need to lower its frequency. When you explore the world of feeling leading to the experience of virtue or higher values, the experience of the body–mind–feeling unit is one of vibrational exaltation, or Light. For some, this experience resembles an expanded body sensation of high-pitched sound. To return to this state, as in returning from some meditative states, the frequency is lowered (densified) by focusing upon bodily sensation itself. The physical body acts as a neutralizer. Another way of accentuating physical density (or the process of densification) is through certain kinds of breathing or movement that involve the body itself. So endow the thought form with your physical experience. This means incorporating it, literally joining it to the corpus, as if you were putting it on like a garment.

Sense, feel, and see the consequence of your desire made manifest in your own experience.

Take this a step further into your silent meditation. There it will be endowed with soul substance as you raise and release the desire unto the world.

22. *Visualization*

These last two exercises, while also including the use of spiritual faculties evoked through visualization, concern two fundamental practices for every woman.

A. CLEARING AND CLEANSING

Offer your actions to God and to Its expression as Mother. Before going into the dark womb of the night, thank life for all the experiences of that day, regardless of how these may have appeared to you.

Create a prayer to recite every night, knowing that whatever you hold in your mind as you enter into sleep will be taken with you into the higher dimensions and energized. Thus the purest-quality Light fills you and returns with you to your world in the morning.

At the end of each day, gather the energy related to whatever images haunt your mind or issues still remain unresolved.

Visualize them being absorbed by a radiant golden sun in your midriff—just between the diaphragm and the lower belly. See and feel this golden disc rotating, loosening, and sucking all discomfort and heaviness from you, especially all fear or anger.

You can send the disc down into the earth or visualize yourself handing it over to some angelic presence who will reabsorb, re-qualify, and dispose of its contents.

Now visualize another radiant golden-white sun there, filling up the space where the fear was.

Ask that the following day allow you to know, and to be more and more your self.

Before going into sleep, construct the appropriately realized thought forms for the following day. *(These may be a successful interview, the healing of a friend, the completion of a project. . . .)*

B. BLESSING

Within your usual meditation practice, when you've set up the space, aligned yourself, invoked, generated, circulated, and made the necessary calls. . .reserve some time for the experience of silence—of feeling without content.

From the fullness of yourself, send out oceans and oceans and oceans of love into the world. Remember that Love is not an *emotion*; it is a *state of Being*.

You may visualize this state as sending forth pink doves, or heart-shaped balloons, smoky energy, or whatever other shape you wish. . .infinitely expanding.

You can also concentrate upon a particular place on the Earth that needs Love.

You will notice that you become ever more charged doing this.

Alternatively:

Find a very quiet, discreet place among as many other people as possible. This can be on a hill or a large meadow, a cathedral, or a gathering.

Impersonally and imperceptibly, embrace all those people. Wish them well. Wish that they received the help, guidance, inspiration, and lift that they need right now.

Be sure that nobody notices, and that you tell no one.

This final exercise involves your humanity and the wholeness of yourself to identify with the two basic archetypes that live within each woman.

23. Transmutation: Healing The Magdalene Wound

In spite of her training, the Magdalene suffered bitterly at the foot of the cross and wept disconsolately. The eruption of her emotions was the all-too-human "failure" to put emotions aside. This is the "Magdalene Wound," the death cry, as impulse, that comes from the entrails of the Earth when it feels its children suffering, when nothing seems to make sense because the love that has brought meaning is no more. If only temporarily, the experience is one of sustained emotional agony.

Through introspection, go back over your life and identify your greatest emotional pain.

Take in all the associated feelings and thoughts.

How do you feel you "failed"? How did you not live up to yourself? How did you lose your dignity or purpose?

See the circumstances and people involved.

Remember other scenes of similar distress, and take note of your actions and reactions. . . .

As you look around you. . . .is there anyone who was hurt, or confused, by you at that moment?

How were different people affected by your behavior?

Allow yourself to remember the mixture of guilt and yearning. . .that it would have been different.

Hold that feeling, and let it pool within your heart.

There is nothing to do but feel.

Allow associations to flow into your mind even if they are not connected to you directly: scenes of great injustice, of war and famine, of natural disasters that broke your heart -all the more because you could do nothing about them.

Feel the sorrow of unimaginable, untold, unfinished things, secrets, moments of shame and remorse, that women have shared through the ages.

"Oh, if only. . . !"

Feel how your heart is heavy.

You long to reach and heal and change it all! Hope never dies!

You have located the place of the Magdalene Wound—a deep pain nothing, and no one, can quell.

Nothing can make you forget. Nothing can fill that space.

It is pure impotence, and it presses upon the heart that sinks into a pool of spinning, bottomless endlessness. . . .

Now look beyond yourself. *You* know the place. Take your prayer up, up, up. Raise your arms and take the feelings up, as if in taking flight towards the heavens, the infinite possibility you know exists, without knowing how you know.

Wish with all your heart for the righting of all that has caused suffering in the world.

Feel the Mother enfolding you, just the way Mother Mary embraced the Magdalene at the foot of the cross, even while her own son suffered.

Feel the presence of pure love.

You are both the Magdalene and the Mother.

See and feel billions and billions of tiny particles of Light, like golden snow floating through space, descend upon you, falling like nectar of golden sweetness over you— absorbing density and darkness.

Your tears become tears of gratitude that your heart can contain it all.

Feel loved. And safe. Everything is as it always was and will be.

Part Three

Empowerment
And Application

THE OPENING IS THE REWARD

Mother,
you come so softly I hardly notice
the scintillating shimmering of tenderness,
silent, invisible,
never imposing, always embracing.

You surround me with your breath
and fill me with your sweetest sound,
Presence in my emptiness,
certainty leading out of darkness and despair.

Mother dear,
you bring confidence and courage
in depth and height,
in absence and in fullness
everywhere
eternal womb of All That Is.

As Binah
in dignity and Truth
you reveal the sacrificial Eve,
the glory of Lillith before fear,
purity and wholeness which in its blackness
contains the seed of Light.

And now I know
I am your daughter
and all the children of the future
returning home complete,
in beauty and faith unbroken.

Your sacred form upon this holy, holy Earth.

IN THE HEART OF THE WORLD

IN EXPRESSING HERSELF in the world, women must master both male and female characteristics. The active or positive state requires we use and handle force: initiating and leading, guiding, creating, performing normal tasks. The receptive or negative state calls for connection, flow, and response, for synchronization with inner forces, rhythms, and dynamics. No matter how efficient, intellectual, or political we are, we remain women executing what are largely considered male tasks. Conversely, when we carry out female functions, we do so in a manner qualitatively different from men who perform the same task.

Power, and degree of consciousness, are attributes of spirit; form and quality apply to embodiment and gender. Spiritually, men and women are equal and consistent throughout the individual evolutionary chain; in our physical bodies, we are, however, different and mutable, alternating gender, race, and so many other characteristics. The palette offered through gender tones and soul frequencies presents an ample spectrum of combinations and possibilities for experience.

Embodiment is tinged with the tonalities of soul—implied but not always visible. A strong, fiery, and forceful quality, usually masculine traits, may be found in a female who may not exhibit such characteristics overtly. Exquisite tenderness and emotional receptivity, normally female characteristics, may be found in a male who is nonetheless masculine in his worldly expression. Outer expression serves to add to the irradiation of soul.

As an example of soul quality, consider Jesus, who incarnated as a male in a world ruled by men. It is reported that he was so beautiful and magnetic that he enthralled, not only women, but also men. He incorporated soul qualities that, at the time, appeared as essentially feminine values upon the Earth, but he did this through a masculine polarity. So too did the sensitivity of a St. Francis of Assisi, the tactful, embracing mind of Gandhi, and the Buddha demonstrate soul characteristics typically attributed to women.

It is not as easy to understand and intrinsically accept masculine values reflected through a woman. Joan of Arc, Ayesha, Mohammad's warrior wife, and Hatshepsut, a passionate woman who loved deeply while also ruling as a pharaoh, are examples of this phenomenon. A woman cannot easily reflect her strength and leadership ability without being pegged male-ish. It was all right for Mother Theresa, whose field of activity was that of a caretaker, and for other prominent women in fields like ecology, education, and women's rights. Consider, however, the criticisms suffered by Margaret Thatcher, Madeleine Albright, Hillary Clinton, and Angela Merkel in their careers.

In each generation, women strive to make their mark; and today, more than ever, this is the rule rather than the exception. Examples of marvellous women abound. We can only ask ourselves how the Magdalene would be today, or Mary the Mother of Jesus? They might be a mixture of Florence Nightingale, Indira Gandhi, our ordinary housewife, and Mother Meera. We need to take a little from each remarkable woman, including Brigitte Bardot and her passion for saving the animals, Katherine Hepburn's spunk and tenacity, Mother Theresa's persevering dedication, Amma's inexhaustible love, and Golda Meier's organizational skills. A woman incorporates the electrifying perfection of strength and material execution exquisitely, but she also transmits something else, a fragrance that affects all but remains unseen and intrinsically unrecognized.

Simply put, through our intuitive access to the higher mind, we balance and complement feeling with intelligent activity in a way that is also *emotionally efficient*. The Great Mother expresses herself as ferociously as she does tenderly and intelligently, with an acute perception of the future. She is visionary. She is considerate. She is egalitarian. She is freedom. She is real wealth and knowing. Her abilities match her resources. Her scope matches her breadth and depth. She lives and generates the starlit magic and majesty of the Creator as the shape of pure Love *in the world*: universal, cosmic, eternal, and earthy.

In the Orient, the way of woman is likened to the power of the moon rather than the sun. Taoism calls this "the Watercourse Way," denoting the steady streaming feminine power of water that inevitably overcomes the brute force of stone. Similarly, the moon in its pervading magnetic activity saturates, dilates, and remolds the entrails of the Earth in the darkness of night, bringing death so that rebirth and renewal may occur.

The moon is dark and cool, like the Mother. The sun is bright and hot, like the Father. Curiously however, although both are equal in their wholeness, the moon depends upon the light of the sun. That is its *way*, just as the way of the sun is to shine and project impartially. The moon has no light of its own but rather absorbs and reflects the light of the manifest sun and transforms it, *altering the very quality of the light,* that humankind may feed from it. As the sun gives us life electrically, so does the moon blend and cast its filaments magnetically into the lower worlds and material life.

Mother dresses us in the clothing of moonlight as holy, spiritual substance, that we may play the game of creation and handle the very elements of her domain, that we may learn mastery and dominion as women and awaken, from the inside, the heart of our fellow men. In silence and serenity, we fuse with the Mother as our incarnated birthright to then collaborate and merge with the Christ force. Together we express God's Love, power, and authority over the body of humanity and the texture of the generations to come.

But first, as women we must, as She does, enter into, through, and beyond the darkness of the night that harbors the light in the heart of the world. We must re-enter the womb to find it. We must till and water the soil and then, in the twilight of patience, see the flowers bloom in divine justice and perfection. Then, with perfect timing and consciousness, we follow their perfume into the heavens. There, within the Love-light thus perceived, we co-participate in the birthing of stars and suns and millions of moons. . .as Light upon light! And stars and moons and a billion suns sing ecstasy throughout the ever expanding sourcing of all life.

The guided practices in this last section help us embrace the experience of integration of human and divine, cosmic, and planetary forces, and male and female expressive aspects within us, by taking us directly into forces within matter, feeling, and thought. These practices train and develop awareness, focus, and management of energies to evoke, sustain, and apply energy frequencies in our world.

These attributes are not always integrated, which is why traditional alchemy and high magic are faculties common to enlightened Man, whereas in divine alchemy and conception, we witness the consciousness associated with realized Woman.

1. My Body, The Whole

In the three-dimensional world of experience, the personality manifests needs in order to master vitality in its many forms. In the same way that a man needs a woman (lover, mother, teacher. . .) to find himself emotionally, a woman needs a man to define herself in the physical world (lover, father, teacher. . .). This is the way we learn to collaborate.

You can only be what you are. When a man allows himself to embrace his male instinct for physical conquest and domination without exploiting it, he makes the space for the feminine in him, because he knows and feels safe in his own power. In strength he also has the power to be vulnerable (feminine) without threatening his identity. His body knows what it is to be the custodian of the Earth, the father of humanity and future generations, and it knows instinctively what it is to govern and to set norms, to open ways, and to preserve. Cellular memory is his guide.

When a woman dares to embrace her vulnerability, her opening to life and existence, her womb, her body, and her emotions in contact with the Earth, using her seductive powers and attractive magnetism with awareness, to enfold and to feel the intuitive magic that occurs within her as receptivity and processing of life's energies, she invariably taps into her strength as force, her masculine source. Her body knows what it is to be mother, lover, educator—naturally, perfectly. Cellular memory is her teacher.

Now, let's see how we can hold a serious and heartfelt dialogue with our own bodies as women. You should spend a whole day, at least, meditating on this next practice.

Your whole body form is your anchor. You don't need to visualize roots going into the earth. Your whole body *is* the Earth.

Feel your body as a whole, including weight and density, volume and quality.

Sense what it wants to do and be. What it says and feels. Resist emotional interpretations, and stay with the sensation of the body.

Sense its rhythms: when it wants to move, and how, or to rest.

Sense the pulsation of parts, and distinguish them from the frequency of the whole as an organism.

Discover how you *relate* to your body through your thoughts and feelings, your desires and impulses. . . .

Neutrally see and feel all impulses—good and not so good— originating from within you.

Feel the forgiving grace of the very Earth as it enfolds all those feelings and sensations with its love. It doesn't stifle them. These are your own—your offspring.

Sense now the different textures and elements within your own body, the play of weight and movement.

The angles and spaces formed by your bones, the muscles, and flesh.

The orbs traced by the life of your organs.

Intuit it, all of it, giving you form and volume and qualities of energies. (*Through inner vision and feeling, you may perceive different colorations, tones, densities and movements. . .*)

All of Nature, her moods and cycles, her seasons and her every gesture as rain, wind, sun, and soil. . .her passionate inten- sity as storm and her serenity as clarity. . .her peacefulness and her readiness for hope. . . .

Be the planet Earth. Lend it your life, your love, your feeling, your sensation.

And now bless it as only you can. As only the Mother can. Thank it for its service to you.

Your Consciousness sets everything alight. There are now

billions and billions of tiny suns of all colors, shapes, and circuits within you. They speak of Father Sun and Mother Moon. They know the story of Creation and of life.

Raise and intensify that love into ecstasy now!

Stand within this marvellous universe, in proud yet humble admiration for the beauty and bounty of Creation, a creation that is a part and apart from you.

A. HOME

Woman is the Earth, but this does not always translate into being grounded. In fact, most women are afraid of their power and the surplus of sensitivity it bestows. So they avoid the fullness of experience their body grants them, space out easily, become hysterical, and delude themselves at every turn. Woman needs to touch and be touched. When we can define ourselves physically, we become solid as the Earth.

In daily life we love handling detail. We like things. Even if we are not the type to like fashion or, perhaps, don't concern ourselves all that much with personal appearance, we always have one area in which we focus our appreciation for form. It may be horses, horticulture, antiques, a collection of little boxes, or even the way we arrange our drawers or set the table. It could be just that one object that we treasure immensely.

Often we also treat our body parts—fingernails, hair—or those of our lover, or even those of our baby, as things. This is by no means demeaning, because we exalt them to the height of supreme beauty. We marvel at shape, color, textures . . .with our natural sensuality, coupled this time with our fascination for form, a form, of course, which we unconsciously sense we lack.

This guided meditation is given here for the home, but you may change and use it as you please. As you do naturally, now do consciously, delighting in the play of textures, color, and lines in order to ground yourself as you beautify your surroundings.

This is a standing, walking meditation, touching, and pointing to different objects of the home.

Sense the volume and weight of your body as you walk around.

Arrange the way that you walk so that you feel your full sole on the floor (*or earth*), and your body is sensed as a whole. This means that you may become aware that one side is heavier, or that there is a split between your waist and belly.

As you take this in and scan your body, recognize how your mind redistributes the sense of mass inside your own body. (When you occupy the lighter or emptier space inside the body with your mind, this automatically becomes heavier or denser. A certain balance occurs that leads you to ultimately occupy the full body equally.)

Now, stand still and feel your feet in contact with the ground. Sense the Earth's energy, the Mother's body, breathing, pulsing . . .and resonating with your own.

Feel the Earth's energy rising through your legs, and bring it up to the belly.

Tune into the heavens now, and feel the energy descending. The quality is very different.

Bring the energy from the heavens, which you sense as light, through your head, flooding it with light, and down into the heart.

You now feel two distinct qualities: the Earth energy centered at the belly, and the cosmic energy centered in your heart. Hold this for a few minutes, and take notice of each kind, as you define your connection with the source above and the source below you.

Become a passage of energies.

Open your arms, and allow both energies to intermingle and flow out through your hands.

Now, walk around again and examine the space you live in, the things that fill it.

Allow your feelings to come up. You may see something old and tattered that was very beautiful once and gave you much pleasure.

You may see something you've dutifully kept but never liked very much.

You may come upon objects that are dead because you never paid attention to them.

Now you wish to honor them, all of them. Qualify them with the energy *you* wish to have in your home.

Pick up an object, any object. Allow your appreciation to come out through the sense of touch.

Feel it with your fingertips, your whole hand. . .bring it to your cheek if you will.

Sense your energy now rising from the belly to join the heart and, from there, stream out through your hands and fingertips.

Become aware of this flow, and consciously intensify it, feeling that you are flooding this object with appreciation.

Pick up more and more objects, and impregnate each with your personal feeling.

Even the ugly, lifeless pieces you could never rid yourself of . . .find something beautiful there.

Fill all the rooms of your home, requalifying everything in it.

As you touch, become aware of how your energy flows into the pieces. You may visualize it as stardust or light beams with specks of dust. . .pink-golden dust.

Become aware of how you are a qualifying vehicle as the energy comes from the earth and up and out through you, and from the heavens and down and out through you, acquiring each time the quality that you call for.

Touch. . .caress. . .the things in your home until you see them shining bright. As each piece glows, you too glow, amplifying your heart's delight until you are a sun-presence there!

Now, do the walls and floors, the big surfaces. . .

To the places you can't reach with your physical touch, send this energy forth from your fingertips or through your sight.

See the ceiling, books, bookcase, closets, cupboards, all covered in the rays of light that you emit. . . .

Qualify the totality of your home as a place where light abides, a worthy temple for God's priestess. . .a place of rest and healing grace for all who come here.

Train yourself to do this specifically each time that you clean, or each time that you come home. Come home.

Additionally:

While cooking, charge the food that you prepare.

While eating, see the light within each morsel.

While showering, enrobe your body in golden liquid light, or pink, or blue, or green.

While bathing, immerse your body in a tub of liquid violet, or blue. . . .

Touch *life* everywhere you go with reverence, imparting your quality into it, that all—animate and inanimate—may reveal the light.

Know it. Feel it. Be it. And it will be so.

B. CONSECRATION OF MY PHYSICAL BODY TEMPLE

Form the habit of communing with your body and its parts, so that, whenever anything is out of harmony, you may tend to it immediately, before it becomes illness. As you learn to decode its language, you will also be able to perceive others' dis-ease before it becomes disease, especially your children's. Teach them how to heal themselves.

At night, before going to sleep, in your prayer of thankfulness for life and the experiences of that day, dedicate a few minutes to each organ and part of your body. *(It is under the care of archangelic intelligence but responds favorably when you address it in its own language— the language of love and light.)*

Begin with your feet. See them sparkling white light. You might want to consecrate them by placing a cross within a circle on the sole of each foot, or a star—preferably an eight-pointed one.

Move to your legs, and take into account each part: the calves, the knees, and the thighs.

Each part has something to say. *(The calves represent your potential, the knees your sustaining power, and the thighs your holding capacity.)* Love and thank each.

Go now to the pelvic area. Sense the cradle as it holds the trunk of your body. Feel the opening of the vagina into the womb. Go right into the depths of it, as if it were a holy cavern.

Reverently visualize a candle there. Pray that its white light will purify and heal all matter and substance.

Observe the tonalities acquired by that white light. *(Take special care that the light reaches into all the crevices. Feel and see the walls of the womb glowing with a healing violet hue, following that with pink or gold.)*

Extend that activity to include the intestinal tract.

After a while, you will notice scintillating pink-golden foam begin to spread from the very center of each atomic particle. Watch it grow and absorb all negativity, all toxicity.

Be filled with this light, now a lavender with golden-pink, as it consumes and requalifies your pelvis and intestines, radiating out through the whole pelvic basin, into the ovaries and up through the intestines, shooting backward as well into the lower back all the way up to the waist.

Seal the area with a large equal-sided cross inside a circle, or a five-pointed star.

Address yourself to the liver, and from there work yourself out to include the stomach, kidneys, pancreas, and gall bladder. Thank and bless them for their service to you.

Repeat the previous procedure, taking care to intensify the candle flame so that it swells up high into the thoracic cavity.

Center yourself in your heart. Talk to it just as if it were a delicate child, or a flower.

Use a pink flame here, and watch this organ absorbing every bit of love that you pour onto it.

Soon you will see another flame being emitted from the heart. Within a diamond-like casing, three tongues are detected: pink, blue, and golden.

This is the seat of your soul.

Be sure you approach each color frequency separately. Thank your heart and your soul for all human experience. Bless your heart, and seal it within a six-pointed star.

Feel the energy from the candle at your womb, now accompanied by the glorious light at the heart surging upward and diffusing a violet glow through all the parts of the body. Notice how the light within each part obeys you.

Direct yourself to your lungs.

When you are done, its billions of little sack-like pockets will be sparkling in all colors—like Christmas lights. Rejoice at its beauty. Bless it, and seal it with the cross within the circle.

Go to your hands, and include the arms and shoulders.

Visualize the light-center of each atom responding to the cleansing process, blazing white.

Your hands, arms, and shoulders become radiant white. Thank them for serving you so well, and place the seal on each palm. *(Unless this is specified or another option given, this is the equilateral cross within the circle.)*

Pray that all you touch may be soothed and healed, and impregnated with the light from your Consciousness.

Your throat deserves special attention. *(You might like to try spinning your own symbol here, or a nine-pointed star, and watching how it clears away all accumulation of spoken and unspoken words and concepts.)*

Allow the heart flame to rise higher and higher as it soars right past the throat and gives off healing, peach-colored irradiation.

Seal it. Consecrate it to the service of the Light: that all your words empower only Truth and Love.

On your head you should work on two levels: your face, and the central point of intelligence in the center of your head.

See your face and all your features. Thank them for serving you, and cover them with the sheerest veil of starlight.

See this veil now over your complexion as it feeds your love right into the cells. See your face perfect as it is. Pray that nothing disturb its harmony.

As you feel the inside of your head, visualize the gray matter of your brain becoming pale gold, pushing out all toxicity onto the surface to be cleared.

Allow the heart's flame to rise higher until it ignites another flame, right in the center of the head.

Notice how this flame is different. It is made of many colors, spreads up through the top of the head, and falls down into a diamond coat over and around your body. Thank it for the intelligence, awareness, and consciousness it grants you.

Follow the cascading rain of multicolored light over your physical form, and bless it all again, this time as a unit. Feel and see this light feeding and caressing your skin.

Direct yourself to your breasts, those eternal symbols of your femininity, and see them saturated with light. The energy appears as spirals here, culminating at the tip of each nipple.

As you breathe, exhale the natural sweetness that is yours through each breast and notice what coloring you emit.

Feel your entire body surrounded by a shroud of scintillating, diamond glitter forming an armor of light. Feel safe, secure, and above all grateful to life for its gifts of love. For extra protection, when you go out into the world, you might like to visualize dark blue armor like a second skin.

C. THE WOMB OF LIFE

Sense your hollowness, the opening of which is your physical womb, the fathomless depth of it like an inviting abyss, the vortex of creation. There lies a subconscious pool of lower life-forms, seeds of collective humanity in all possible ways. . . .

Feel the power to contain and to embrace life, to blend, yield, and bring forth substance. Offer yourself to the builders of form.

Feel your purity, your eternal untarnishable virginity, the creative Holy Spirit. . .and the pure power of life, the *shakti*!

All imprints and all forms are in your divine womb. You are the ever-conceiving, gestating memory of cellular and cosmic life.

2. Depth And Amplitude

The vitality or bio-energy we expend in our normal activities is gross, kinetic magnetism imbued with sexual force. It comes through as physical stamina, emotional yearning, and a peculiarly conditioned, outer-oriented frame of mind. It is that which we use in living our daily lives. We give it quality.

Soul or spiritual energy radiates through the whole of the personality (including the body unit) but is much more delicate. It cannot express itself, or be detected, while we continue to pump up and manifest the grosser instinctive impulses exclusively.

As women, we never lose contact with the subconscious. Rather than this being a curse, it is a blessing. Every month, through menstruation, we merge and commune with the depths of life. There we become healed, are made whole again and charged with the raw magnetism that we qualify and then express in the world. Even beyond the lunar cycle, every woman disappears within herself at different times to reconnect subliminally with the womb of life.

Our emotional depth and amplitude transmits the qualities of our soul in the world. If we have not explored these depths and come to conscious management, we cannot provide a vehicle for soul to express itself. From the depths of life's activity, we emerge like the phoenix out of the ashes to soar into the heavens.

Once we have become conscious of our personality and refined it, we make space for those quiet murmurings of genuine intuition, and the subtle currents of our soul qualities become more apparent.

We need to free ourselves from preconceptual aggregates passed on to us before we can commune with life directly.

Your belly is a primeval pool of feeling. In depth and amplitude, it houses the inexplicable textures of sensation and the play of emotion, like waves. . .nuclei of subtle, sentient forms, concentric vortexes in perpetual motion, that ebb and flow around you.

Feel this unqualified sourcing within your own body and distinguish it from purely sensorial radiation. It is the feeling of feeling.

Feel yourself as an emotional reservoir of all possible feelings.

Feel yourself as the whole of this activity and also its parts, the many and the one.

Through your feeling network, sense how your body, your feelings, and your mind perceive the activity. Now come to terms with emotional power. Notice how it works, how you participate in emotional manipulation* both as a receiver and as an emitter.

See how each feeling, each emotion, each sentiment works and what it means to the whole. Ride its depths and heights to uncover the anguish, the compulsion, the urge to give, hold, bring close, and unite. . .to set free, to heal, and to beautify. Become aware of the need to touch with your feelings.

Now, add your intelligent awareness, the conscious desire that it be good: your qualification.

Raise or expand each feeling into greater and purer expressions.

Do this with the totality of the emotional mantle about you.

Notice the role of thinking in this play: Understand, in this dynamic play, what manipulation, once rendered conscious, can be used for. . .what empowering life is all about! What you can *do* with all this feeling.

Know your rhythms and your relationship with the rhythms

---

*manipulation: *Something shaped deliberately. In this case "manipulation" is merely the handling of force and does not imply a negative activity.*

of the Mother.

Allow yourself to know when to hold and how to sustain, when to liberate, and when to deepen and multiply.

Collaborate with the Mother's feelings for *all* her children equally.

A. MAGNETISM AND GRACE

Sense what your body, your female body, exerts as magnetism, as attraction. This goes beyond sexual attraction to the very root of sexuality as the essence of vitality. It is connected with you as the manifestation of the matrix from which substance arises.

Feel those waves composed of a full range of desires arising from your body.

Now compare them with the grace that your highest feelings produce to inspire and uplift. This is intrinsically linked to Consciousness as receptivity to higher law. It is the crux of your beauty.

Condition those waves to compose a full range of higher desires arising from your soul. Notice the contrast with the unchecked desires of your body.

See how one wave brings energy into you and the other radiates it out—one takes, the other gives. . . . One is personal, the other transcendent.

Follow this rhythm while generating your highest desires. Your body's energy now *serves* the soul. You turn into an instrument of grace.

Allow yourself to freely dive deeply into the innermost recesses of your pool of feeling, into that dark, moist region of the subconscious, the night, your repose, your nourishment.

Feel its fullness and its power. . . .

And now let yourself rise, renewed, from its depths, cognizant of all life's feelings in everything and everyone. And give of yourself, through yourself. . .

Go from substance to essence, diving and rising with the fullness of all life.

3. Empowerment

Yours is the gift of empowering others. This happens automatically through your faculty of emotional attunement. When you do it consciously, you emit a force that allows a person to move mountains. You motivate and incentivize life's forms to manifest their perfection.

This is a quality of our body as a female polarity; energizing the emotional reservoirs of those we become involved with and projecting strength. This intensifies the feeling force that precedes creative endeavor. Be careful not to agitate instead.

As self-originating activity, something entirely different happens. This center, as the solar plexus, is negatively charged in women. We inspire mental activity emotionally but are incapable of generating it in ourselves. We lack categorical precision and consequent clarity in the third dimension.

We use the concrete mind in conjunction with the feeling faculty. Our particular brand of doubt is indecision and insecurity, something that gnaws away at us almost constantly.

Let's now see what we can do about this.

A. DISCERNING AND KNOWING

Examine the process that you normally use to decode your feelings and also to pick up on others' subconscious—in other words, to know what is happening.

The focus now should be on how you arrive at the *right* interpretation.

Distinguish among the following: the *thinking mind*, the *feeling mind*, and the *knowing mind*.

The thinking mind refers to concrete thoughts. These could be a shopping list of things to do.

The feeling mind involves evaluation and pleasure. This consists of likes and dislikes.

The knowing mind is what we normally call intuition, or the voice of conscience.

Combine that knowing mind with the process you normally use for decoding. Hold the intuitional frequency in suspense while you organize your thoughts.

Instead of directing it to someone or something, visualize a sphere of luminosity like a diamond-shining oval. Its outer edge is crystal blue.

Drape this over and around yourself—about two meters away from your body.

Now breathe out into this oval, filling it with breath that you color snow white.

Feel safe and secure within this mantle of light.

Notice now a brilliant star at the place of the solar plexus, made of the same material as the oval. Notice its seven points.

Feel the balancing, harmonizing, purifying influence of this star as it absorbs your confusion, brings you peace, and then dissolves within you.

Now, allow your knowing mind to discover what it needs to know, and translate that into your activities in the ordinary world.

Give yourself permission to explore everything that you need to know.

B. EMPOWERING THE SOURCE

Observe how you empower others, how another becomes strong with you.

Choose someone whom you wish to help, and establish a silent, intuitive connection with him or her. The connection must be at soul level. This means that you can't have a vested interest of your own.

Allow the most exalted expression of love to accompany the frequency of the knowing mind and, tuning into the person's higher self, wish that its highest desires be realized. You do this through *appreciation* and *gratitude*.

Simply and fervently wish them well unconditionally.

You don't need to know how the higher self will use this. It is enough, in this case, to wish him or her well.

This is an exercise in patience and trust, in knowing, and in *holding that certainty in a fixed position* through your own presence. This allows it to be received and used by the other in a higher dimensional frequency.

In time you will come to distinguish the many powers that emanate from the source, through you, for higher purposes, and be able to establish a concrete link between knowing and your illumined concrete mind.

4. The Power Of Light

Whereas, at the previous level, you empowered others emotionally through a kind of projection, here you act on your convictions with the forcefulness of a positively charged heart in the material dimension. Yours is the original manifestation of fidelity and faith as unshaken loyalty and love's determination.

This is the spirit that moved Joan of Arc and allowed her to mobilize all of

France. Nothing can impede the flow and concretizing ability of the female who is ignited by the certainty of her heart. Her body obeys her, and so does the rest of matter everywhere, because it addresses the essential core of life through the female mind, which, as concentricity, envelops the totality of circumstances. In this sense it is the spirit of sublime motherhood that commands, because it is one with what it commands. It knows that it knows.

The holy spiritual power that moves us as women uses our emotional and mental vehicles in order to empower others. It also expresses itself strongly and effectively in a physical way as the force of love at the heart. Herein lies our real power in the world. We project love emotionally and mentally so that others may find and become themselves. Physically, love's force obeys us.

This phenomenon was the source of the courage portrayed by the archetype of Mother Mary when she knew she was pregnant. She possessed the strength to stand alone in the truth of the God-self that lay within, facing society with the humble yet unmovable fortitude that comes from inner conviction. There are not many women who attain this realization and use this power in daily life. It is the epitome of female intelligence compelling activity through the heart, or Light Point, that lies at the center of all creation, the source of divine alchemy.

It is the power of Light. Once in alignment with it, all else must bow before it. Creation complies with the Creator when it has applied the forces of the Mother.

A. DIVINE CONCEPTION

For this journey, you will be invoking archangelic assistance. In order to vibrate at a frequency where you may reach it, you must evoke the utmost purity and selflessness. You may call upon the spirit of Mother Mary and allow her presence and her experience to overshadow you.

Imagine yourself visited by a Being of Light, such as Archangel Gabriel. Feel his irradiation as the ultimate in softness. His tenderness is overwhelming.

Notice the soothing waves coming from this presence, and

its translucent colors: the rose and soft yellows within a predominating sky blue effervescence.

Allow this irradiation to heal deeply, seeping into your pores until it impregnates the innermost part of your body at the womb.

Feel a seed being deposited, as if it were the seedling of the God-child, a holy presence within.

Respond with loving, grateful thoughts. Allow your heart to become one with its heart.

Now, follow the expansion of your heart blooming with a new certainty. It *can* be brave. . .for Him! For the child representing Truth within you!

Visualize this child of the heart as a magnificent white-golden rose, brilliantly glowing and transfiguring your entire body and atmosphere.

Follow its stirrings, and notice your entire body responding with a new impulse.

Now, sense yourself walking through your daily activities with the strength to manifest all the good and beautiful and perfect things that you wish to see in your world.

Return to your daily life, bringing this quality back with you.

Dare to use it. Allow the Holy Spirit to fill you and guide you always.

5. *The Hollow, Hallowing Source*

You exist in the matrix of space, the blanket within which everything manifests. You are the emptiness within all possible forms. Your hollowness is the precursor of form. It is the silent echo that precedes and also follows the word. It is the core of every state of Being and the essence of your knowing.

When your actions are in touch with this core, you will manifest real lead-

ership and be an inspiration. It is at this point where your higher self is able to bestow upon you its maleness as right and inspired action.

This is no longer the activity bred at the heart in response to protecting the sanctity of life. It is creativity itself. It is protectiveness and nourishment itself. It is the hallmark of genuine response-ability.

We intuit this frequency in our worlds through sound and hearing. It is a mother's lullaby and a child's gurgling caress. It is the flutter of wings and the whisper of angels. We can sense it through our own breathing and notice it as flashes of lightning-like inspiration. We feel it strongly through the speech of others as our body responds to tone.

The quality of Consciousness is reflected in the quality of our voice. This is why it is so important that we match voice to our feelings, that we become aware of its sounds and how they affect others, that we harmonize and use our speech consciously as an instrument for peace.

Equally, we should become aware of the music that we crave, and seek to amplify the range to include greater variety. Study the effects of primitive music, classical music of different ages, jazz, spirituals, reggae, and all the popular styles that continuously arise. Explore each without judgment to understand what it seeks to express. Languages, ancient and modern, also reveal specific kinds and levels of Consciousness.

Ultimately, we should be able to ride—as both cause and effect—through all the notes, the highs and the lows, with equal ease, and when we notice discordance or disharmony, be able to bring balance through our own sustained presence within it.

We are the sound that springs from the matrix, as well as the whole of the matrix—the sound that heals, soothes, lifts, and feeds all life.

A. QUALIFYING SOUND

Try saying *thank you* in as many languages as you have access to.

Thank you. Notice the effect of the tip of the tongue behind the teeth on the first part. The explosive "k" followed by the softness of the "you".

Gracias. Open your mouth wide and feel the vowels. Relish the strong "g" and roll the "r". Hold the "s" as it slides into silence.

Merci. Delight in the sound of the "m". Feel the internalized depth of the "r". Delicately release the "ci".

Obrigado. Put your feeling, as into a kiss, on the first part, "ob". Then come out again in the "ri". Be present in the "ga", and kiss again on the "do".

Danke. Give of yourself on the "dan", and then rejoin your innermost self on the "ke".

Ευχαριστώ. Sense the fullness of the movement of the sound as it parts from your depth ("oefff"), makes a full circle through your body ("ka-riiii") and is emitted as a liberating breath of Consciousness ("stó").

Notice the feelings and the energy of each of them. No one is better than the other. Instead, each expresses a uniquely different way of being, just as we do in our inimitable individuality.

Now, observe your ordinary speech, and practice different kinds of intonation. Become aware of the power of the word.

Inject full feeling into your words, so that they go out into the world and produce what you want them to. Each is a different creation.

B. The Motion of Silence

Make a sound, any sound. Then another and another (*let these be nonsense-sounds, without any meaning*).

Now, extend that sound and sing. Enjoy it.

As you sing. . .feel the hollow spaces within vibrate the resonance.

Free yourself to sing beautifully, feeling the vibratory activity of your vocal cords as their sound weaves through different and unexplored regions of your body you never listened to before.

Feel the sounds glide and pulse through your entire body and spread out around you.

Now, become the spaciousness within which sound slides and rises.

You are the passage through which all impulse flows, the hollowness, the empty space beyond form, the backdrop for creation that links worlds.

Feel yourself as the ever-present state of emptiness available to all potential.

Yield to the impulses. . .and give birth to movement. This is action that is born from inaction.

Notice which movements are spontaneous and real, and which are forced. (*Allow rather than produce the movement.*)

Return to the pregnant pool (totality or formlessness) from which you arise each moment anew, refreshed.

Sing again.

Sing the melody of silence's yearning to manifest the absolute.

Explore this with your speaking and turn each word into a song.

Sing to your children on Earth. Sing to your brothers and sisters everywhere. Sing to the plants and animals, and notice them gently respond with their own song.

Qualify your voice with the brightness of love's fullness.

6. The Vastness Of Mind

We have seen how cognition originates from within the mind of the absolute, or God, touches higher mind, and finally resonates in the concrete, linear mind. By virtue of the female mind, we are linked directly to the wisdom of the absolute through intuition, often without the intermediary bridge of the linear of abstract process. Although this remains indeed a gift, it is more often a curse. We want to know, see, and measure what we literally swim in, but rather than in orderly precision our mind responds by leaps and bounds.

We create with equal ease through our peculiar mind as we conceive through our body. Our third eye is positively charged, which means that we project thought forms* effortlessly charged with mind substance* without mobilizing or employing the mechanisms of deduction and construction that men access. Our feelings become thoughts instantly. When unguarded and untrained, these often hover around us in great, cloudy profusion. However, with practice, they serve as blueprint for the construction of a better world.

Ours is the power of true mediumship. Once we hone our perception, we are able to distinguish what pertains to physical, subtle, or spiritual expression.

We perceive the whole and embrace time instinctively. To experience the present as cascading, simultaneous activity at different levels is natural, for the simple reason that we are not tied to linear reality. We conceive Being and non-Being—the seed, the flower, and the fruit—together. Not only this, our inner nature does not give up in the face of ugliness, violence, or defeat. In this way, we point to the transcendence of the human and the realization of the divine.

A. THE MIND OF THE WORLD

Attune yourself to the mind of the Mother, the female mind.

Be engulfed by her.

Use your inner senses to commune with her: see, feel, touch,

---

*thought forms: *Images or symbols constructed through our thinking, and colored by emotional desire.*

*mind substance: *The etheric substance of mind impressed by the resonance and shape of thought forms.*

smell, and taste. . . that silent throbbing present.

Become this everythingness, everywhereness, as a continuous *waiting*.

You are the Mother's priestess—pure presence.

Anything can happen at any moment!

Fire yourself awake and into undiluted alertness.

You are the innermost essence of every form.

Feel the impulse as urges arising. They are the myriad possibilities of form in gestation.

Resist doing anything yet.

Wait and watch and see and feel.

Let all that momentum accumulate within you. Embrace it.

Pray:
"There is a time for everything,
and a season for every activity under heaven:
a time to be born and a time to die,
a time to plant and a time to uproot,
a time to kill, and a time to heal,
a time to tear down and a time to build,
a time to weep and a time to laugh,
a time to mourn and a time to dance,
a time to scatter stones and a time to gather them,
a time to embrace and a time to refrain,
a time to search and a time to give up,
a time to keep and a time to throw away,
a time to tear and a time to mend,
a time to be silent and a time to speak,
a time to love and a time to hate,
a time for war and a time for peace."
—*Ecclesiastes 3: 1-8*

Feel these cycles of activity as you embrace them all in the now.

Greater nature lies within you: summer, spring, fall, and winter. . .life, death. . .birth, youth, maturity, old age. . .Being and non-Being.

Time is an unmanifested part of you now.

Sense probable dimensions existing as unexpressed aspects of you.

Remain serene, impartial, objective...

Notice the colors that spring from you as a source. They acquire form and density, sound and resonance.

You are the divine medium, knowing, communing, and accessing all possibility.

You are elevation and transcendence.

Be the golden radiance that now surges outwards from your divine formlessness.

You are the mind of the world feeding on itself and unfolding into the textures of reality.

7. Source Of Cosmic Light

Woman's soul contains the movement that generates light continuously. Our womb is the outer manifestation of pure receptivity; and our creations, including human life, are the expression of Light.

We receive as much from the heavens as we do from the Earth. Whereas a man fecundates us with the seed of physical matter, which will construct the human form, the heavens impregnate us with the sacred fire that represents the Consciousness that will live inside that form.

We remain the means through which the absolute channels nourishment and Light-substance that become its powerhouse.

At every moment we have the choice of identifying with matter or with spirit, responding to the laws of physics or to the laws of grace.

Divinity multiplies through us, as the Mother. The universe expands in a sea of Consciousness that we unfold from within ourselves. We know how to produce light, to manifest, amplify and accelerate the very universal Life within life, universal Light within light.

We know the experience of peace and the transcendence of opposites. We are the very altitudes and profundities of ecstasy. We are both fullness and emptiness. Oneness is our nature.

Our brother is Love's expression in all possible worlds. We mirror his soul, his breath, and represent the Love that feeds him. Together with him we are the Unity that is God.

A. FULLNESS BEYOND EMPTINESS

Allow yourself to merge into the great silence that pervades the presence of Light.

Blend all colors, all differences within yourself.

Now spread yourself out into infinity and timelessness, filling the universe with your presence.

Feel the fullness that is your birthright.

Beatitude.

Complete, whole now.

Be.

B. DIVINE CHANNEL

Within the fathomless eternity of the cosmic universe, feel the presence of the Father calling you.

Attune yourself to His sound, His frequency.

He is heralded by legions of angels and many different light forms. See them all and be filled with each one as they surround you

Be very, very still.

As He approaches you, your feeling form becomes more and more transparent and yielding. . .until you become all light and welcome Him into you.

Nothing else exists—only pure luminosity and a buzzing, humming ocean of light particles.

Transfer this to your physical body now, and feel as if His hand is upon your head.

His touch releases streams of diamond light through you.

Be that rivering course of cosmic light.

See it feeding the Earth through you, its mountains, valleys, waters. Feed the children, the plants and animals, all God's creatures.

Nourish all of life!

Remain in this state of grace for as long as you wish, yielding to the Father and assuming the role of the Mother.

Upon returning, notice how the diamond light acquires more volume and density, becoming a milky-pearl elixir.

Become a cup filled with this bubbling, scintillating nectar of immortality.

Feel this sweet cascade descend into your human form, saturating it and flowing out through your hands and feet.

Bless your feet, and hands, and consecrate them to the service of the Light.

Take your stand now—declare that whatever you touch, wherever you tread, you will bring relief, hope, and renewal.

c. God Within

See your physical form at a distance of about three metres from you. All white, it is composed of billions and billions of tiny suns, points of light.

See a larger body now, a replica of the first and extending from it. It is made of light as well, but is more diaphanous.

Now see a third body, larger than the second and enclosing it, made of an even more radiant quality of light.

See the three bodies overlaying one another, blending and harmonizing. . .the larger giving to the middle body, the smallest receiving from both.

Now visualize a ray of light descending from above and suffusing these bodies. It is brilliant, brilliant white.

As it comes into contact with the bodies at their base, it ignites into a flame. From within that flame rise three tongues of fire!

The whole looks like a crystal jewel, with pink, blue, and golden strands that concentrate at the middle portion, around your heart.

The three flames merge and combine and, with tremendous explosive joy release vivid greens, orange, purples. . . .

The activity intensifies as fireworks that pulse with life and shine in all directions.

It goes on and on and on.

Now, look at your bodies again and notice, one at a time, where the focus of sacred fire lies in each one.

The largest body has this focus on the head. See how it feeds the third eye and seven flames arise, forming a crown, sowing intelligence.

In order to perceive the second body, you must lower your vibration slightly.

Its center appears in the region of the heart. See how it glows and grows and spreads wide, creating beautiful orbs of soap-bubbly rainbow hues, awakening love.

And now, tuning into a slightly lower frequency, observe your vital body. The sacred fire nucleus shows in the region of the solar plexus.

See it feeding vitality to your organs and maintaining them in perfect health. Notice its lightning-like effect as it flows out and pulses through your body, releasing a glow through the skin as well, feeding you life!

Now see all three bodies again, and bring them toward you. Allow them to dissolve into the body of physical matter that you wear.

Feel your body again. Feel each repository of Light.

You are the guardian of the sacred fire, eternal vestal virgin. . . daughter of Love, Mother of Life.

Then As Now...

Our real individuality, like our real self, is both defined and indefinable. It is a quality that manifests through our life's expressions, including our personality. It is irrevocably unique within a range of possibilities, acquiring form within archetypal expressions of the higher spheres, and flowing through personal traits.

What we are can never be entirely expressed or understood in our three-dimensional form. We are what we have always been, pure Consciousness. What we appear to be, and how we express the body that we wear, however, can be seen, formed, and defined. Personality is something different—temporary, concrete, and malleable.

Therefore, the personality is the spirit's vehicle. Either it blocks its expression and causes pain and suffering, or it widens to reveal the miracle it encloses.

The Female Sage

The ancient wise one: She is old beyond years. She knows it all. She has seen it all. She has done it all. She has had it all. She has made her peace with humankind. She has made her peace with the Earth. She is ready to face the Creator with the wholeness of a life lived fully. She can wait forever. Or she may leave tomorrow...

Evoke the archetype and go inside it.

Feel your body.

Know your feelings.

Acknowledge your thoughts and the vast inclusiveness of your experience.

Contemplate your children, grandchildren, great-grandchildren.

Look around you at the Earth.

Conceive of the seasons, the all and the everything, with impartiality and kindness: the seed, the fruit, the flower. You know. And you know that you know.

Gather all the fruit of your living.

Remember the games you played, the darkness of despair, the joys, the victories, and the lies—big and small—that you told yourself when you were young and wanted to believe in them.

Recall the hopes and dreams. . .and see how in a strange way so many of them came true! Even beyond your wildest dreams.

The perfection: Look around again at the young. Smile at their folly, and remember your own.

See the pretentiousness, maybe even the manipulations, of the adults who run the outer world, and the secrets, their secrets. As if they could hide anything from you! And you smile because you know that, in time, they too will know.

Listen to the complaints of the old, with their frail bodies and their unlived dreams. Hear the cry of the sick and the rebellious who abused their bodies and denied the Mother.

Embrace everything within yourself.

And look before you.

Now let yourself speak from that love and wisdom that has been your life. . .speak to the children, to the young, to parents and the adult world, to the old and the infirm.

Share yourself with each and all of them as only you can, from the fullness of yourself.

*Now. . .*now feel the gratitude of the Earth.

Then the Mother calls you back unto her agelessness. Feel Her surrounding and enfolding you in Her grateful, gentle night to take you, sweetly, reverently, back home.

Rest now in the breast of the Mother-Father absolute all.

As It Was In The Beginning: A Prayer-Meditation For World Understanding

For this final practice, use everything you learned. Prepare yourself, delineating each detail, each form and sequence, carefully. You may use a lighted globe of the Earth as a prop and select the music that inspires you most. Be sure that it evokes the depths as well as the heights of human feeling, the amplitude and the ecstasy of Light in all its expressions. You will need to apply both male and female mind faculties.

Align and center yourself. Dig deeply into the Earth. Sustain your consciousness in oneness with the planet.

Now raise your consciousness, connecting the weight and volume of your body as Earth, with the heart center in Love.

Be this Love to everything. Condition it so that it continues by itself as you move your linear thinking elsewhere.

Invoke the downpour of divine grace, the fullness of mind or the descent of the sacred fire. You may do this through the recitation of a prayer or the declaration of a decree.

Ignite the thought with feeling and sensation.

Hold it, in perfect silence and serenity—without any desire.

Condition it to irradiate by itself as fullness and joy.

Now qualify this fullness with understanding. Direct your intention, as prayer, that there be understanding and acceptance of truth within the hearts and minds of everyone.

Fervently desire that all may become illuminated and, in doing so, understand the causes of disease, suffering, and the general chaos and violence unleashed upon the world. Take care, as you do, not to allow any feelings of hatred, guilt, fear, blame, or sorrow to interfere. Sustain the hope that inspires a new course of activity and opens the way for it. Take your time in setting this up and then in sustaining it.

Hold the irradiatory frequency of pure love and joy, and the now-qualified consciousness of understanding which you wish to instil.

Conceive of exactly *how* people will awaken and understand how they attracted these conditions, how we are all indelibly linked into the planetary unit, the human race. No one can rise or fall without taking everyone with them. Pray that they realize the futility of revenge, possessiveness, and separation.

Want it so much that you actually feel your heart embracing and containing everyone within this state of loving, feeling understanding.

Allow your heart to feel the heaviness of all that is not that love. Allow it to "break," feeling the pain of this condition.

Go right through the heartbreak into fullness again. Allow yourself to be the transmuting agent for all that which is not the purity and perfection of the beginning. You may repeat this step as long as you feel it is necessary.

Evoke unity, respect, brotherhood, eagerness to work and collaborate, animating, visualizing, and feeling the activity of each as something happening within you.

Actually see all these things taking place all over the planet.

See people receiving them and acting upon them.

Visualize the healing of humanity take place.

Witness the healing of illnesses, the making whole of children and adolescents, and the caring of the elderly.

Now, leap into future time and conceive of a world where understanding and peace reign.

Think of the men, women, and children of the future. Conceive of how they would think. Conceive of how they would feel.

Feel it as within yourself.

Create the pattern for that future *now*.

Allow yourself to know God's plan: Perfection as it was in the beginning, is and will be, in the realms of Truth and Light.

Glory to God in the Highest and on the Earth. . .Peace.

MOTHER	DAUGHTER
You work in darkness and in silence.	Angel of my Light! Precious perfume of Love's fulfillment!
Your deepest lessons are given in inner chambers where no one goes.	Your becoming exudes the fragrance of Realization: as Woman, as Love, as Spirit untainted.
And no one knows but you. . . the Light that grows inside me.	Incarnation of Ideals. Breath of Godliness. Inspiration. Starlight Wings.
	The dove of Ultimate Peace flies free upon the petals
No one knows.	of your flowering.
I Am That.	*I Am That.*

IN A BETTER WORLD men and women will work together to evoke, construct, and preserve the harmony in the world. Harmony means peace. We are in harmony with ourselves when we acknowledge, accept, and transmit Source, when we embody it through our physical, mental, and emotional bodies fully. Only then can we merit the attainment of harmony with another and within the world. Only then do we earn the right and all the powers to create it.

We have come of age. We no longer speak in terms of commitment between just one individual with another. The divine marriage involves all of life. It speaks of the great Tao between heaven and earth. It also happens within us, women.

Ours is the power to heal humanity of hatred and despair. Our reverence for the source of our own Being as women, leads to using this most precious expression wisely. Only the transcendence of corruptibility within us can ensure the continuity and the uplifting of the human race.

Women are the blood of life, that flow that runs through the veins of life everywhere, as birth, death, and resurrection. We can only pray that we become each day more worthy to receive and sustain those frequencies of pure sourcing through us, which transmit and multiply Light upon the Earth.

As absorbers and emissaries of the divine Light, we rule over darkness and the firmament. Like the Egyptian goddess Nut, we offer our bodies as a blanket for the night so that upon its velvety dark softness, the stars are revealed. We are the ever pregnant darkness which contains the Light. We bring balance back into nature through the embodiment of the principle of blessing sustained. We birth the future, bearing the message of hope and renewal.

APPENDIX

The Inspiration

As I set out to write this book, behind the familiar Golden Lady of my childhood appeared Mary, the Mother of Jesus. She was the very first archetype of a feminine deity my mind conceived so long ago, and was as vivid then as she had been fifty years before. It was to her that the child, the adolescent, the young woman, the parent, the teacher and the crone within me addressed: "What *is* Woman?"

At first Mother Mary didn't speak and seemed to work at me hauntingly through a gnawing expectancy. She seemed to say, "Address yourself to Mary Magdalene. She knows."

The Magdalene! She had frightened me. At that age, in that place, at that moment in time, she wasn't the kind of mother a little girl would seek. But I was older now, and she was too evident within me to deny.

And then each one slowly lifted the veil behind which I had kept them.

Dual Aspects of the Mother

VIRGINAL GRACE

At first, this is a field of energy, and then slowly a human form emerges. . . .
She comes like the soft presence of morning after a jet-black night. Before you know it, you are filled, as if from the inside, by a joyous depth that feels like emotion but is fullness itself—the presence of Love. Her presence quells any fear, takes its place.

Unless your heart has been stretched by the experience of living life undivided, at the core, you might sense her energy as pain, as your heart expands to make room for her. For her to be able to reach you, she must resonate as wholeness at the very depths, those regions beyond despair and helplessness experienced by the heart as it learns to love.

Her voice is every voice, and every sound, and the essence of every word. . .because it is the presence of Love's intelligence. She cuts through every qualification with the force of that silence that speaks of everything that can possibly be said, because it knows the end—the end of all life's lessons.

She stands serene and soft, acquiring consistently greater definition. Her look sharpens at once into crystal purity and depth. There is no lie, no pretension, no illusion that could withstand those eyes. Strong and tall, there is nothing frail or inconsistent about her. No act, chore, or activity could ever be beneath her.

Her movements of mind, as of body, are deliberate and grounded. Concentration and precision are blended with sensitive, extended perception. She sees it all, knows it all, and has a perfect sense of timing. As Mary, she had an art for taking one point at a time and helping us to accomplish the most complex tasks in orderly perfection, never absent, never late. The full stance of Mary, as she was in the times of Jesus, is both noble and humble at the same time, almost invisible and also imminently close.

Always quick to embrace and comfort us, her sense of humor is like a coaxing that jests us into seeing ourselves in a greater light. But she won't be manipulated or bought by deceit and pretence, waiting until the right moment, when it has faded, before speaking, touching, or coming near.

As Mary, she was trained in every conceivable esoteric practice. But she also brought the innate knowledge of archangelic irradiation with her into the human form. Unlike the previous Egyptian cycle of austerity in focus, Mary incorporated discipline and depth of perception tempered by the flexibility of the human, feeling nature. Anchored in divinity, her humanity was also spontaneous and natural.

Even at the foot of the cross, she never cried—not the way we cry. Yet in daily life her eyes were often filled with tears, feeling for everyone, and knowing. . .knowing beyond their grief. Hers is the sustaining grace that held Jesus during the most harrowing ordeal at the cross, and accompanied Him through the inner planes. It was for this that she was born. And long after, she possessed the posture and the keys for immediate access into the realms which her son had reached, moving easily within dimensions of Being and time, and teaching this to all around her through transmission.

It was she who housed, embraced physically and spiritually, baptized Maria of Magdala, and prepared her for the ways for woman in the ages to come. While the Magdalene had the physical experience of the world, Mary the Mother had the emotional and psychic correspondences that united the human with the divine. Alone, or with a disciple, or in the company of this daughter of her heart, she travelled extensively throughout the known world of the time, physically seeding, in people and places, what would germinate in the cycle to come.

Today she speaks to every human heart who calls to her, instilling patience, fortitude, and hope. She is the Mother as Durga, Lakshmi , and Parvati, who listens and loves, unconditionally, enveloping us as devastating softness in a mantle of effervescent rainbow light. These colors are the flowering of the seeds she plants, blossoming and issuing forth the perfume of myriad expressions of mature humanity. We are held within her aura of absolute infinite Beingness as Mother. . .for all eternity.

Experience Of The World

I turn to Mary Magdalene, the enigmatic character of early Christianity, the central figure for sinners as well as saints, seasoned by the toil of human experience and naturalness. I ask her to reveal herself. She permeates the field of my perception as both forcefulness and tenderness. There is a shyness to the boldness I now intuit. . . .

The colors are strong and vital at the periphery, with soft pastels radiating from the core and again at the outermost edges of the energy field. You feel immediately a gnawing sensation at the heart, almost an irritation but more like purposefulness, a determination to exist and manifest and be and give. . . . But strangely, this issues forth from hollowness at the core, an overwhelming and pervading experience of emptiness. Hers is the courage of a broken heart that learns to live.

Her voice is melodious. Deep, resonant waves seem to caress the skin and hair. . . . It is a tender, nourishing sensuality. But it can also be provoking and ravaging. As Shakti and all her expressions, including Kali, she knows how to soothe and heal the harshness away, or to inflict it under the wings of love, to awaken and reveal. Her actions speak as loud as her words—often piercing and direct, a no-nonsense straightforwardness that even the strongest shy away from, and she remains an indefatigable ally to the women she teaches and has led since time immemorial.

Mary Magdalene appears extraordinarily beautiful, well educated and charming in any circle. Some say she was a courtesan, others that she was a priestess of the old ways but that she also owned a confectionary business. She loves children, making sweets and making people happy. We see her before Jesus when he first touched her and revealed with that touch the previous experiences in esoteric schools. Multidimensional passages open, and she not only understands who it is who has touched her but embraces as well the perfection of the circumstances of her life, her relationships and behavior leading up to that pregnant moment in time. And then we see her dancing and laughing at the wedding feast of Cana, radiantly happy with Jesus. She personifies at this point the greatest love that any woman could ever experience.

To see her walking in the marketplace, often with the blessed Mother, we might admire her lithe graceful movements. She is quick in step as in wit, swiftly vanishing when she doesn't wish to be found. She might be called a split personality today: melancholic, vital and intense, incorporating the moodiness and darkness of Persephone's realm. She is seen everywhere with Jesus and Mary as the sister-disciple and daughter-apprentice, and as the leader of the women. She would found the first convent in old Antioch.

As I see her now—bright refined features, dark shining eyes like the depths of an ancient river, tall with billowing hair—she stands both defiant and vulnerable, a profound sadness in her gaze. Men and women are drawn to her wisdom and passionate intensity, wanting to be touched and taught by her, seeking her protection as well as her human warmth and palpable understanding. The Magdalene knows people both psychologically and energetically. She knows the art of blending and merging, feels people's pains, shares their dreams and also delves within their fears with them. . .so much so that they often become her own. She seems to absorb and become them, eventually transmuting them within and through herself.

She loves deeply, with all her human faculties and spiritual nature wrapped up into one peaking intensity. Unafraid of demonstrating her love and affection for men, women and children, she is the overall woman of all. She revolts against categorization, standardization, and masculinization, injustice and distortion, with the fierceness of her loyalty to truth.

At the foot of the cross, the lover-sister-mother-friend is all too human. And it is there that she makes the mistake that every woman is apt to make. Impotent and profoundly involved in the human experience surrounding her, the adept turns away from higher grace to identify with the prevailing human condition. She embodies the indulgent excesses of emotional woman. At that moment, the seal of her broken heart, as the "Magdalene Wound," imprints not only the heart of the women who are under her care but also the existential female helplessness.

What has been written nowhere, but indelibly engraved within our hearts as women, can now be read. Together with the promise of a joyful future in the resurrection, the racial memory of the Magdalene Wound reveals the shadow of defeat. But the cross of suffering and darkness that has long been projected onto her is disappearing. As she travelled extensively in the world of her time, she also planted seeds in the hearts and minds of her followers, and these are bearing fruit today. For this she returns, calling to women everywhere to transform emotional force into the power of Consciousness.

You are seduced by the power of that love to arise and be your self.

The Woman Of The Future

Mary's grace and the Magdalene's passionate intensity, Mother Mary's spiritual power and Mary Magdalene's conscious management of energy in the physical world—this is what this book is all about. The Blessed Mother was chosen for her purity and unwavering presence. The latter, who was a priestess and a teacher, the embodiment of divine alchemy, was chosen for her capacity to *know, feel,* and *embrace* mankind. The Magdalene represents the right kind, and quantum, of energy at the precise moment of divine transmission that produces a leap in consciousness. We need not live life in the manner that she lived it, but we must live it as fully and as deeply as our own life circumstances naturally call for. And then we must learn to sustain the fullness and the experience of life in its totality.

The energetic legacy of Mary Magdalene as an archetype includes the wisdom and the presence of the Blessed Mother who taught her and permeated her. She is the divine vehicle for the purification of the subconscious—the example and application of Love in the world. As an early Christian leader, we can only imagine how hard she tried to prevail over the domination of the male mind. . .how desperately she attempted to raise women's conception of themselves, as well as woman's image in the world, and how impetuously she sought to instil the supremacy of compassion over instinct. Hers was a battle we, as intelligent women, are still fighting.

Only experience builds consciousness, as this is created

through fusion with substance of Light and with physical matter. The dynamic involved in the transformation of human consciousness, which is our task in this cycle, involves the conscious use of that which we already are and do. Our role as women is to generate a sufficiently high quality of energetic substance that will enhance the quality of life everywhere.

Any woman who embraces herself spiritually and energetically knows that the real art of loving, including lovemaking, lies in the quality of emotional emission. To be effective, we must transmit caring and warmth. To be really successful, we must genuinely feel this warmth and energetically enfold and contain our loved one, as well as each and every one of our creations. No technique could ever replace this. When it happens, we transmit healing grace and inspiration. We become the emanation of Love. Herein lies our formidable power to nurture and to influence our world.

As heiresses of the Mother's wisdom, women must develop the abilities to:

1. Contain and sustain high intensities through the full experience of Love in action
2. Understand and use intelligence as reason to requalify emotional energy into higher expressions, such as forgiveness and virtue
3. Lead and teach others by example and orientation, which includes the conscious awareness and management of energy
4. Align ourselves with That which Is the essence of Love, as transmitters of the Christ-force

Seeking the sublime Mother as realized woman, the Blessed One of Pistis Sofia. . .the one whom Jesus chose to carry the message of hope and resurrection to the world, we discover women's lost humanity. We find the one who holds the keys to both wisdom and grace, intelligence and Love—the real and eternal woman within every woman.

The Magdalene is the personification of our attributes, both limiting and irradiative. As women, we carry her pain and her joy. We have suffered her humiliation and faced the incomprehension of humanity. We've experienced the degradation of feeling and intuition as common emotionality over the intelligence of the heart. We have also loved as she loved—it might be said, too much. She is every woman. Not only she who weeps, who mourns, who loves as profoundly and as sublimely as is possible, but that other one, the one we don't hear enough about, the one who thinks deeply, who comprehends truth and human nature, who possesses the transcendent, inspiring intelligence of realized woman—who delights in making others happy.

This is her time. This is your time.

ABOUT THE AUTHOR

ZULMA REYO was born in Manhattan of Puerto Rican parents. She travelled widely with her parents in Latin America and attended schools in Puerto Rico, New York and New Jersey. She attained her B.A. in Romance Languages and Literature from NYU in Washington Square, specializing in French, with a subsequent M.A. in Education.

Because of her travels and the diverse relationships that have marked her life, what distinguishes her might be best described as an in-depth understanding of the nuances within emotional climates, and the subjacent nature of people. In her interviews she calls her life a salsa, replete with dramatic heights, depths, and dance modalities.

Postgraduate studies led her to embrace psychology and counselling in the late '60s, while practicing with he whom she calls her "real" teacher: Arthur Janov, author of *The Primal Scream*. He gave meaning to her already curious and sensitive nature through a phrase attributed to his own methodology: "Feel it!" "Feeling it" has shaped her life as much as it has her work. She helps people to feel with their whole body, mind, and spirit, leading them to a breakthrough and connection to the innermost Self.

Like many people, she has woven together her experience with people, places, teachers, and teachings, including the Lucis Trust and the White Lodge College of Psychic Science, a prolonged period contact with an Indian guru, and a residency at the Chicago headquarters of the "I AM". Her training covers body techniques and healing, gestalt, psychosynthesis, Rebirthing, and spirit rescue. Parting from the premise that all practices must stem from the one pervading dynamic that rules human expression, she uses techniques and practices as tools in the service of her own brand of work, called "Inner Alchemy".

After many years of travelling the world, she now lives in Palma de Mallorca, Spain, where she offers trainings, individual work, and conferences worldwide.

She is available at *www.zulmareyo.com*.

ACKNOWLEDGEMENTS

WITHOUT THE SUPPORT of my friend, Dolores Mihanovich, her acumen, good sense, unreserved loyalty, and truthfulness, I would not have been able to do much of what I have been able to do in this world. In this particular case she served as inspiration, sounding board, and demonstration of what a woman can be, not only because she sets herself out to do it but because she already is what she can become: the multifaceted expression of the Great Mother.

Further acknowledgement goes to all the women in Brazil who lived this material in weekly study groups for years and who gave their utmost to further the manifestation of the divine Femenine Principle within and everywhere.

More recently and more to the point, an example of strong female incorruptibility was given by my friend and student on the North American continent, Eugenia Koukounas, who doggedly reviewed and scanned the manuscript with keen curiosity and unfailing detail to make it more understandable for a wider audience, injecting her own brand of clarity and beauty with it.

Finally, a word for my editor-publisher, Barry Sheinkopf. Here's a man who loves us and appreciates us, who doesn't seek to change, use, or possess us, a sensitive artist who dares to look beyond the surface. Thank you, Barry, for seeing us as we are and for believing in us.

This book has been set in Hoefler's *Requiem*, derived from a set of inscriptional capitals appearing in Ludovico Vicentino degli Arrighi's 1523 writing manual, *Il Modo de Temparere le Penne*.

Lightning Source UK Ltd.
Milton Keynes UK
UKOW04f1338021013

218352UK00001B/27/P